D0907361

POLLINATOR CONSERVATION HANDBOOK

POLLINATOR CONSERVATION HANDBOOK

Matthew Shepherd

Stephen L. Buchmann

Mace Vaughan

Scott Hoffman Black

The Xerces Society

Portland, Oregon

In Association with The Bee Works

The *Pollinator Conservation Handbook* has been edited by Michele Glazer and designed and produced by John Laursen at Press-22. The typeface is Stone Serif in various weights. The 200-line color separations were created by Jim Haeger at Revere Graphics. The books have been printed on recycled Endeavour Ultra Dull by Millcross Litho, and Smythe-sewn and bound by Lincoln and Allen.

The Xerces Society
4828 Southeast Hawthorne Boulevard
Portland, Oregon 97215
www.xerces.org

ISBN 0-9744475-0-1

Acknowledgments

This book would not exist without generous contributions of time and knowledge by many individuals, and we thank all of them for their guidance. Expert review was provided by James H. Cane (bees), Carol A. Kearns (flies), Jonathan R. Mawdsley (beetles), Robert M. Pyle (butterflies), and Lynn Wilson (education). David Johnson read and commented on early drafts. Special thanks go to Charles D. Michener, who reviewed the entire text and honored us by writing the foreword.

For the photographs that grace these pages, we are grateful to Arthur Evans, David Inouye, Jeff Owens and, in particular, Edward S. Ross. Ed has been a great supporter of the Xerces Society for years and we are always proud to reproduce his photographs.

We thank Michele Glazer for her skillful editing of this handbook. Over many hours she patiently coaxed explanations and clarifications of technical subjects from us and melded four disparate writing styles into a single voice. We also want to thank John Laursen of Press-22 for designing the book and overseeing its publication. John has been a good friend of the Xerces Society for many years and is largely responsible for the high quality of this and other Xerces publications.

The contribution made by each of these people improved the book. Any mistakes that remain are the responsibility of the authors.

Publication of this book has been made possible by the generous support of Metro, the United States Fish and Wildlife Service, the National Fish and Wildlife Foundation, the Meyer Memorial Trust, the CS Fund, the Richard and Rhoda Goldman Fund, the Dudley Foundation, the Grant High School Octagon Club, the Turner Endangered Species Fund, and Turner Enterprises.

Finally, we are particularly grateful to our wives, partners, and children for their tremendous understanding and patience during the months we spent researching and preparing this book.

Foreword

Science and common sense tell us that species exist in an extremely complex web of interconnections such that, when a single species is removed, scientists cannot always predict the consequences. However, there are natural interactions between species so fundamental that the loss of one of the species will clearly be disastrous for the other. Pollination is one such process.

Most flowering plants are pollinated by animals. If pollinator populations are depleted, many of these plants will produce fewer seeds or no seeds at all, thus failing to reproduce. The result is that plant populations are weakened or disappear altogether.

The *Pollinator Conservation Handbook* describes how you can help protect and re-establish populations of pollinators that are diminished or locally extinct as a result of human activities.

The most common and important groups of pollinators—bees, flies, and beetles—are also most prolific and diverse in somewhat disturbed areas where they can find bare ground and sunny stretches of woodland edges. Since people have created many such disturbed areas in the name of "progress," you might think there would be more bees. However, we have gone much further and—armed with pesticides, weed killers, earth movers, and asphalt—we have occupied or degraded so much habitat, destroying nesting sites and floral food resources, that pollinator populations are threatened.

Pollinating insects are essential to our gardens, to most of the earth's flowering plants, and to human beings who are dependent, like every organism, on the web of life. This handbook will help you learn how you can provide the habitat that pollinators need to thrive.

Charles D. Michener
Watkins Professor Emeritus of Entomology
University of Kansas, Lawrence

Contents

Pollinator Conservation Handbook

1

Introduction

In the Hawaiian Islands, biologists rappel down sea cliffs to reach and pollinate plants of 'ōlulu (*Brighamia insignis*) and pua'ala (*Brighamia rockii*), two species that would be extinct without this human intervention. In California, the endangered Antioch Dunes evening primrose (*Oenothera deltoides* ssp. *howellii*) survives on only a few acres of degraded sand dunes; it lacks pollinators and so produces only a fraction of its potential seed crop. The rare western prairie fringed orchid

Insect pollinators are necessary to the healthy reproduction of over 80 percent of the world's flowering plant species. Edward S. Ross.

(*Platanthera praeclara*), scattered across grasslands of the midwestern United States, is now visited by a species of moth that is not native to the habitat. This moth fails to pollinate the flowers because it can reach the nectar without touching the pollen and, furthermore, it drinks nectar that might otherwise attract hawkmoths with shorter tongues, which are the orchid's legitimate pollinators.

This alarming pattern is being repeated around the globe. As the insects that many native plants require for adequate pollination disappear, the effect on the health and viability of these native plant populations can be disastrous. And that's just the beginning.

Pollinators are keystone species, that is, species upon which the persistence of a large number of other species depends: they are essential to the reproductive cycles of most flowering plants, and thus to the ecosystem itself, supporting plant populations that other animal and bird species rely on for food and shelter. Pollinators are also indicator species, meaning that the viability and health of pollinator populations is a good marker of the health of the ecosystem of which they are an integral part.

The *Pollinator Conservation Handbook* focuses on North America. Native bees are the pre-eminent pollinators here as, indeed, they are world-wide, and it is with particular alarm that scientists from nearly every continent have been documenting dramatic declines in their populations in recent decades. In China, for example, fruit growers are pollinating flowers by hand because pesticide use has killed the bees in the orchards. Similarly, in Britain, rare orchids survive because biologists are doing the delicate work of transferring pollen by hand; the bees that pollinate these plants are locally extinct because their nesting habitat has been largely destroyed. In fact, nearly two-thirds of Britain's twenty-five species of bumble bees, once the common denizens of hedgerow and pasture, are in decline. At least one, the short-haired bumble bee (*Bombus subterraneus*), has not been seen since 1998 and is considered extinct in Britain.

Three factors—the loss and fragmentation of habitat, the degradation of remaining habitat, and pesticide poisoning—account for

A mining bee (genus *Andrena*). Bees are essential pollinators
the world over. Edward S. Ross.

most of the declines in populations of native bees and other native
pollinators. These factors have complex political, economic, and social
origins and ramifications that are not easily addressed. But at another
level, the solutions are simple and straightforward. Many insects are
fairly resilient, and there are actions we can take in our own back yards
and neighborhoods, on farms and ranches, and in city parks and wild
areas, to help strengthen and support pollinator populations.

The *Pollinator Conservation Handbook* is a comprehensive guide for
gardeners, farmers, ranchers, educators, city park managers, and public land managers to assist them in providing, enhancing, and managing habitat for pollinator insects. Also included are ideas for developing school curricula, as well as an extensive list of resources. The
Handbook contains practical and specific information on how to establish flower-rich foraging patches and nesting sites for pollinating
insects any place where there is space enough for a few plants, whether
it is a backyard patio in Bangor, Maine, a golf course in the suburbs of
Chicago, school grounds in Birmingham, Alabama, or field margins
in rural California. Your efforts on behalf of pollinators will, in turn,
help maintain healthy plant communities in wild lands and support
bountiful harvests on our farms and gardens.

2

Pollinators: Why Care?

Cut an apple in half by slicing across its middle and you will find a central compartment in the shape of a five-pointed star. If the apple has two seeds inside each point of the star—ten altogether—it was perfectly pollinated by bees. If there are fewer than ten seeds, not enough pollen reached the flower's stigmas to develop all of the seeds because there were not enough bee visits. A poorly pollinated flower will develop into a distorted apple that is smaller and lopsided—and thus considerably less appealing to consumers—than fruit resulting from fully pollinated flowers. And an unpollinated flower will not develop into an apple at all.

THE ECONOMICS OF POLLINATION

Consider for a moment that approximately one out of every four mouthfuls of food and beverage that you consume required the presence of a pollinator. The United States alone grows more than a hundred crop plants that need pollinators. Without them, there would not be apples, pumpkins, blueberries, and many other fruits and vegetables. The economic value of insect-pollinated crops in the United States in 2000 was estimated to be $20 billion. If this calculation is expanded to include indirect products, such as the milk and beef from cattle fed on alfalfa, pollinators may be responsible for the successful production of almost $40 billion worth of agricultural products each year.

In the Pacific Northwest, for example, pollinator-dependent crops are a mainstay of the agricultural economy. In Oregon and Washington they are concentrated in three agricultural sectors: fruits and berries, alfalfa, and vegetable and flower seeds. Oregon ranks first in the United States for harvest of blackberries, loganberries, black raspberries, boysenberries, and youngberries. Washington ranks first in the United States for apples, sweet cherries, and pears. Both states also produce substantial crops of vegetable and flower seeds that are completely dependent on good pollination, and both are major producers of alfalfa, a plant whose seed production is greatly enhanced by pollination. In 2001, the combined value of these pollinator-dependent crops was nearly $2 billion.

In addition, pollinators are directly or indirectly responsible for many of our medicines, dyes, beverages, and fibers (especially cotton and flax). In short, flowering plants are the basis for much of our food,

We can thank pollinators for the successful production of as much as 25 percent of everything that we eat and drink—crops that are worth $20 billion per year to the U.S. economy. Stephen L. Buchmann.

our physical health, and our economic stability, and pollinating insects are essential to the life cycle of flowering plants.

BENEFITS TO NATURAL AREAS AND ECOSYSTEMS

The work of pollinators has value beyond the clearly economic. Pollinators help keep plant communities healthy and able to reproduce. In many areas pollinators are crucial for both herbaceous flowers and shrubs; indeed, almost all of the arid Southwest's bushes and smaller trees—such as mesquite, creosote bush, and chamise—are pollinated by bees. When the pollinators are lost, the effect may not be immediately apparent. In fact, bushes and trees may continue to flower and look normal for decades, so that by the time it is noticed that they are not reproducing, it may well be too late to reintroduce a pollinator and preserve the ecosystem.

In the case of rare plants, it is only by identifying and understanding the habitat needs of their pollinators that we can even begin to assure the plants' survival. The endangered dwarf bearclaw poppy (*Arctomecon humilis*), for example, grows only in the Virgin River Basin of southern Utah. The flower's dedicated pollinator—a minuscule bee, *Perdita meconis*—was finally identified nearly a decade after the plant was listed under the Endangered Species Act. Until that identification had been accomplished, conservation efforts could focus only on protecting the habitat of the plant but not on providing for its other ecological requirements.

Pollinators not only pollinate flowers, they help plants in other ways as well. The tunneling activities of ground-nesting bees, for example, improve soil texture, increase water movement around roots, and mix nutrients into the soil. Beetle larvae in dead trees help them to rot, returning the nutrients locked away in the tree back into the soil to be used by other plants. The larvae of many syrphid flies eat plant pests. And so on.

In some areas, pollinators support plant communities that in turn bind the soil, thereby preventing erosion and helping to keep creeks

Some plants and their pollinators rely on each other for survival. In Utah, the endangered dwarf bearclaw poppy (*Arctomecon humilis*) is pollinated only by one species of bee, *Perdita meconis*, which in turn collects pollen only from the poppy. Stephen L. Buchmann.

clean for fish, mussels, and other aquatic life. Mammals ranging from red-backed voles to grizzly bears depend on pollination-derived fruits and seeds, and about a quarter of all birds consume as a major part of their diets the fruits and seeds that result from animal pollination. Even more directly, bees, flies, butterflies, beetles, and other pollinator insects are important food sources for birds, lizards, and spiders, and as such are central to the overall health of the natural community.

Pollination is an essential ecological process, and pollinators are fascinating animals. But the real imperative behind this book is the fact that, as with most wild creatures, pollinator populations are declining as a result of human activity. If this trend continues, driving whole populations of pollinators to extinction, the result will be disastrous not only for the insects, but for humans as well. The purpose of this handbook is to offer tools—information, understanding, and practical suggestions—that will help us begin to reverse this trend by providing and enhancing pollinator habitat and by helping people become more aware of how our actions affect pollinators. But before we elaborate, it will be useful to first understand how pollination works and who the pollinators are.

How Pollination Works

Dust-like pollen grains, the vessels for the male gametes (a plant's male sex cells) are produced in an anther, the swollen tip of a stamen. For a flower to be fertilized and seed to be produced, pollen must be transferred from an anther to a stigma, the sticky tip of a style, a stalk-like extension on the top of a carpel. Collectively, the stigma, style, and carpel form the female structures of a flower, known as the pistil.

The number of stamens in a flower varies from just a few to dozens. In some flowers, like those of wild roses, apple trees, or cacti, they can be seen as a ring at the base of the petals. As with stamens,

For a flower to be pollinated, the pollen grains must move from an anther to a stigma. In this cactus flower, a mass of pollen-covered anthers cluster around a single, taller style, which is tipped with stigmas. Stephen L. Buchmann.

a flower may have several pistils, which are often located in the center of the flower, within the ring of stamens. When a pollen grain reaches the stigma, it germinates and sends a microscopic tube down inside the style, carrying the gametes to the plant's ovules within the carpel. Once fertilized, the ovules become the hard seeds from which new flowering plants will grow.

The movement of pollen from anther to stigma—pollination—is central to the life cycle of flowering plants. Movement of pollen from male to female parts of the same flower or to another flower on the same plant is called self-pollination; movement of pollen between flowers on different plants, however it is transferred, is cross-pollination. Although plants can produce seed from self-pollination, cross-pollination is necessary to ensure a healthy plant community. The transfer and mixing of genes occurs when pollen moves between plants results in generations of more vigorous plants that are better able to thrive in a variety of conditions.

Since flowering plants are literally rooted to one spot, they have evolved ways—being carried by wind, water, or animals—to achieve pollination. The pollen of some plants, including grasses, conifers, and a few herbaceous plants such as ragweed, are carried great distances by wind. The likelihood of the pollen reaching a productive landing is not great, so the blossoms of these plants produce millions of grains of dry powdery pollen to be carried on the breeze (and cause misery for hay fever sufferers) in order to reach even a few stigmatic targets. Pollen transfer by water is used by a very small number of aquatic plants, such as seagrass and water starwort. Like wind pollination, this method requires a great quantity of pollen and a strong element of chance to succeed.

The majority of flowering plants—more than 80 percent of plant species—rely upon animal pollinators to carry pollen grains from flower to flower. Because animals transfer pollen more efficiently than wind and water do, plants that are pollinated by animals produce pollen in smaller quantities; but these grains of pollen are larger and have rough surfaces that help them adhere to pollinators.

Pollinators visit flowers for many reasons, including to find food or a mate. The insects on this common camas lily (*Camassia quamash*) are beetles except for one bee. Mace Vaughan.

ANIMAL POLLINATORS

Pollinators are hungry animals looking for food, usually sweet nectar and fatty, protein-rich pollen, to feed themselves or their young. As they feed, the pollen grains stick to their fuzzy bodies and are rubbed off when they visit the next blossom. Across the globe, pollinators range in size from such minuscule insects as the fig wasp, which weighs a tiny fraction of an ounce, to ten-pound Madagascan lemurs. While the number of pollinator species is unknown—estimates vary from 130,000 to 300,000—by far the greatest number are insects.

Bees are the most important group of pollinators. With the exception of a few species of wasps, only bees deliberately gather pollen to bring back to their nests for their offspring. While bees do not, of course, gather pollen with the intention of pollinating plants, they do, in the process of foraging, transfer pollen from flower to flower. Indeed, a female bee may on a single foraging trip visit thousands of flowers, transporting pollen the entire way. In contrast, butterflies, flies, and beetles visit flowers to feed on nectar (or on the flower itself, in the case of some beetles), and only the pollen that happens to stick to their bodies is transferred to another flower. Bees also are inclined toward "flower constancy," meaning that they attend to a particular plant species on any given foraging trip. This is important because pollen is wasted if it is delivered to the stigma of a species of flower other than that from which it was gathered.

The *Pollinator Conservation Handbook* devotes considerable attention to native bees, not only because of their importance as pollinators, but because, although scientists know quite a bit about native bees and their importance in the ecosystem, much of this information has not been widely available to the public. Butterflies are also important pollinators, but there are already many resources available about butterfly biology and how to create a butterfly garden. Flies and beetles are significant pollinators as well, but scientists know relatively little about their role in pollination.

Although bees are the focus of this book, we do not address the needs of the honey bee (*Apis mellifera*), despite its importance as an agricultural pollinator. The honey bee is not native to North America and there are questions among scientists regarding its impact on native bee populations. Furthermore, largely because of its value to agriculture, the honey bee has the well-organized support of researchers and beekeepers, whereas native bee populations do not. For more information about the honey bee and some of the questions surrounding it, see Appendix A.

3

Meet the Pollinators

An astonishing bestiary of pollinators occurs across North America. Bees and butterflies may come first to mind, but there are many more, from the merely odd to the completely unexpected. These include species of bats, hummingbirds, moths, beetles, thrips, flies, many of the wasps, and even slugs. Of the thousands of pollinators in the United States and Canada, approximately 99 percent are insects.

The diverse insects discussed in this chapter form the core of the pollinator population in most areas. By understanding their biological needs at various life stages you can help provide the habitat they need for nesting and foraging, thus helping yourself and strengthening the health of the natural world.

INSECT LIFE STAGES

All of the pollinating insects described in the *Pollinator Conservation Handbook* complete a metamorphosis through four distinctly different life stages: egg to larva to pupa to winged adult. Pollinator insects vary considerably, though, in where the female lays her eggs, how mobile the larvae are, and what the insects eat at their various life stages.

The life span of a pollinator from egg to death may last from a few months to a couple of years, and the insect will have specific shelter and feeding needs at different stages of its life, both during the lengthy larval and pupal stages when it is not pollinating, and during the adult stage when it is.

Most bees are active as adults for two to four weeks, but bumble bee workers and non-native honey bees may live longer, typically four

Leafcutter bees (genus *Megachile*) may be half an inch long, although most species are smaller. They carry pollen in bunches of bristly hairs—or scopae—on the undersides of their abdomens. In this photograph the yellow pollen grains can be clearly seen. Edward S. Ross.

to six weeks. Butterflies live as adults even more briefly, usually only a week or two. Flies and beetles have similarly short adult lives. Inevitably, there are exceptions. A few butterfly species, such as the monarch and the mourning cloak, overwinter as adults and thus may live for several months; and some female bees, the queen in a bumble bee or honey bee colony, for example, will live for a year or more.

Pollinator species also differ in their egg-laying and larval food needs. Butterflies lay their eggs directly on or near the caterpillar's food source, which is often a particular species of plant (the "host plant") so that the caterpillars don't have to crawl far for nourishment. Species of flies and beetles vary widely in where they lay their eggs, but it is similarly close to or on the larval food source, which might be rotting wood, aphids, or soil-dwelling invertebrates. Bees, in contrast, deposit their eggs in protective brood cells within a nest. The larvae are not mobile, and the nest mother provisions these natal cells with enough food to nourish the brood.

Knowing the life span and habitat needs of each life stage is important because, if you are going to successfully provide habitat for a variety of species, you must provide a diversity of plants and of nesting and hibernation habitats throughout the year. While it might seem a daunting task to establish habitat that will be diverse enough to meet the needs of so many different pollinators, it is likely that if you create healthy habitat for native bees, you will in the process create habitat for other pollinators as well.

BEES

Asked to imagine a bee, you may hold in your mind a fuzzy black-and-yellow-striped insect feeding in a colorful flower, or a cartoon image of honey bees swarming the head of some hapless person. Many of our images of bees are based on children's books, cartoons, and nature documentaries depicting the life of honey bees. The reality for native bees is very different.

Bees are immensely diverse insects that form an important group within the Hymenoptera, an insect order that also includes ants, wasps, and sawflies. There are four thousand known species of bees native to the United States. Ranging in length from about a sixteenth of an inch to more than an inch (two millimeters to over twenty-five millimeters), they vary in color from dark brown or black to red or metallic green and blue; some have stripes of white, orange, yellow, or black; and some even have opalescent bands. Their common names include plasterer bees, leafcutter bees, mason bees, carder bees, digger bees, and carpenter bees, reflecting the many ways they build nests. Others are named after a particular behavior: sweat bees lap up perspiration for the salt; bumble bees hum loudly as they fly; cuckoo bees lay their eggs in the nests of other bee species; and honey bees, an introduced species, make and store honey.

For an entomologist, bees are distinguished from other insects by their obvious waist between thorax and abdomen, two pairs of wings (a feature of all flying Hymenoptera), biting and chewing mouthparts, and segmented antennae that are long and cylindrical. Look with a microscope and you'll also see that the body hairs are branched, while wasps, for example, have hairs that are not branched. In addition, female bees generally have evolved structures for carrying pollen, either patches of long, stiff hairs (called scopae) on their legs or body for dry pollen, or a pollen basket (a corbicula) of long, inward curving hairs on each of their hind legs for pollen moistened with nectar. Female parasitic bees and male bees of all species do not have such features, because they do not carry pollen back to the nest.

Bees can be categorized in two ways: by whether they build and provision their own nests or parasitize the nests of others, and by whether they are solitary or social species. There are both solitary and social species of nest-building bees. The female solitary bee constructs a nest and gathers food for her offspring completely on her own; she normally dies before her young reach maturity, so there is seldom contact between generations. Social bees live in colonies ranging in size from a handful to a couple of hundred individuals (or more than forty thousand for honey bees), where there is contact between the egg-laying queen (called a gyne by biologists) and her female offspring.

The yellow-faced bees (genus *Hylaeus*) are small and wasp-like, with yellow markings on their faces. They do not have scopae or corbiculae, instead carrying pollen in their crop. Edward S. Ross.

Parasitic bees, both solitary and social, lay their eggs in the nests of other bee species, exploiting the stores of pollen and nectar gathered by their hosts.

SOLITARY NEST-BUILDING BEES

About three-quarters of the bee species native to the United States and Canada are solitary nest-building bees. After mating, there is typically no further contact between the female and other bees as she proceeds to locate, prepare, and provision her nest. That said, there is a range of nesting behaviors among the many solitary bee species. Most solitary bees share a nesting site with others, sometimes in large aggregations or at great densities. For example, in well-established nesting sites of alkali bees (*Nomia melanderi*) two hundred or more females may nest in a single square yard, each bee tending a separate burrow. A few "solitary" species are communal in that in addition to a nesting site they share a common entrance tunnel to the nest, but each female creates her own brood cells. More unusual are the large carpenter bees (genus *Xylocopa*), females of which live long enough

The alkali bee (*Nomia melanderi*) is an important pollinator of alfalfa crops. Distinguished by opalescent bands on its abdomen, it excavates its nests in bare areas of salty soil. Edward S. Ross.

Nearly a third of the four thousand species of bees native to North America nest in holes in wood, often beetle tunnels like the ones in this snag. Matthew Shepherd.

to meet—and share the nest with—their adult offspring.

The location and manner by which solitary bees construct their nests can vary dramatically from one species to another. Just over two-thirds nest in the ground, while most of the others nest in wood or plants. The remaining few species nest in an eclectic range of places, including empty snail shells and pot-like cells that they construct on twigs from pebbles and tree resin.

Whatever the nature of her nest, the female bee creates within it one or more brood cells in which to lay her eggs. She usually lines these cells to protect her offspring and their food supply from drying out, excess moisture, fungi, and disease.

Wood-Nesting Bees

Many wood-nesting species use abandoned beetle burrows (typically those of long-horned beetles or metallic wood-boring beetles) in standing dead trees or limbs, but some chew out the soft central pith of dead,

Leafcutter bees (genus *Megachile*), as the name suggests, use their mandibles to cut pieces of leaves or petals, with which they line their brood cells. Unusually, the brood cell at the right is from a ground nest; the great majority of leafcutter species nest in beetle tunnels in trees. Edward S. Ross.

dry stems and twigs from such plants as elderberry and blackberry. A few have specialized needs: the inside of particular abandoned insect galls, for example, or the hollow stems of the common reed. What all of these nesting sites have in common is that they are dry and relatively warm, and offer protection from predators and parasites.

Most wood-nesting species form their brood cells with materials they collect, such as leaf pieces, leaf pulp, tree resin, or soil. Leafcutter bees (genus *Megachile*) line the whole cell with pieces of leaf or flower petal, using their mandibles to cut particular sizes and shapes to fit different parts of the brood cell. Most wood-nesting bees do not line the entire cell, but simply build dividing walls across the nesting tunnel to create separate brood cells. Mason bees (genus *Osmia*) make these walls with mud or leaf pulp. Large carpenter bees (genus *Xylocopa*) and small carpenter bees (genus *Ceratina*) use wood fibers scraped from the walls of the tunnel to form dividers of "particle board." Other species produce building materials out of their own bodies: the masked bees (genus *Hylaeus*), for example, divide the tunnel into cells using a cellophane-like substance secreted from special glands. Each of these bees uses the same materials to seal the nest entrance when it is finished as they use to line the nest.

Ground-Nesting Bees

Ground-nesting bees dig nests in bare or partially vegetated soil that, depending on the species, varies from flat ground to vertical banks. Inside the nests there is also a range of configurations, from a single short tunnel to complex, branching tunnel systems.

Rather than collecting materials from outside the nest with which to line their brood cells, many ground-nesting bee species smooth the cell walls with their abdomens and then apply a waxy substance— produced from special glands near their mouths or on their abdomens —to stabilize the soil and protect their brood. A few species, such as the polyester bee (genus *Colletes*), secrete from abdominal glands a cellophane-like material to create a complete waterproof lining for the cells, separating them from the soil. Some ground-nesting species, such as tiny *Perdita* bees, leave the cells unlined. When the cell is complete, the bee seals it before beginning another.

The Life Cycle of Solitary Bees

Having prepared a brood cell, the nest mother provisions it with "bee bread" (a mixture of nectar and pollen), lays an egg, then finishes building the cell. When she has completed all the cells, the bee usu-

The small carpenter bees (genus *Ceratina*) nest in hollow or soft-centered twigs. The cells are separated by walls of wood fibers mixed with saliva. To the left is a cell containing a larva; in the center is one with bee bread; and to the right is the resting female. Edward S. Ross.

ally seals the nest entrance and leaves. After a few weeks, during which she may have prepared and provisioned several nests, she dies.

After hatching the larvae remain in their brood cells, passing through four or five stages of development—"instars"—while eating the bee bread left by their mother. To avoid contamination of the larva's food supply, the connection between the midgut and hindgut that allows defecation does not develop until the final instar. The last part of the final instar's development, after it has finished feeding and has defecated, is called the prepupa.

The length of time that bees remain in the prepupal stage varies. While the entire development of social bees may take no longer than three or four weeks, solitary bees may have a year or more between generations, and can remain dormant as prepupae for months during winter or periods of drought or other unfavorable conditions. In general, however, those solitary species that emerge in spring (the blue orchard bee, *Osmia lignaria*, for example) complete pupation by the end of the summer and overwinter as fully formed but dormant

Where good nesting conditions exist, ground-nesting bees can form large aggregations. Here, a mining bee (*Anthophora bomboides stanfordiana*) is approaching a site in which each nest is marked by a short entrance turret. Edward S. Ross.

Ground-nesting bees may remain dormant in the nest for many months. In this *Colletes* nest, four of the cells contain pupae awaiting emergence. Edward S. Ross.

adults. In arid regions, where the emergence of adult bees is synchronized with the infrequent blooming seasons of desert flowers, the prepupal stage of some species will last for a year or more, waiting for rain to spur the plants into flowering. Some of these immature desert bees waiting underground are almost seedlike in their responses to environmental cues of temperature and soil moisture.

The changes from prepupa to pupa and then to adult—and the adult's subsequent emergence—are triggered by a variety of such environmental factors as moisture level and temperature, so that the adults will be active when the flowers they need for foraging are in bloom. Some bees nest deep underground—eighteen inches or more—where the moisture and temperature of the soil do not fluctuate noticeably. The southeastern blueberry bee (*Habropoda laboriosa*) is one such bee; though it is not known what cues the bees use in these stable nest conditions, they emerge just as the blueberry plants they forage on begin to flower.

Foraging of Solitary Bees

When foraging, bees are searching for two things: nectar for energy, and pollen for the nutrients it provides for their brood. Solitary bees

Not all bees are black with yellow stripes. This metallic green sweat bee (genus *Agapostemon*) is foraging in an Arizona poppy. Edward S. Ross.

usually collect nectar from any flower whose structure allows them to reach the sweet liquid. The range of flowers from which bees can gather nectar depends upon the length of their tongues. Short-tongued bees can drink only from open flowers such as asters or daisies, while long-tongued bees can reach the high-energy nectar offered by deep flowers such as bluebells or lupines.

Bee species vary in how particular they are about where they collect the other component of their diet, pollen. In general, solitary bee species are "polylectic"—floral generalists who will gather pollen from many kinds of flowering plants. Because their diet is so varied, polylectic bees may be relatively adaptable to changes in plant communities and degraded habitats.

Some species are more selective. "Oligolectic" bees collect pollen from a small group of closely related plants, perhaps a single plant family or genus. The aptly named squash bees (genus *Peponapis*), for instance, specialize on the pollen of squash and pumpkins. The seven U.S. species in the megachilid subgenus *Lithurgopsis* gather pollen only from cacti. *Diadasia* is an interesting bee genus because different species are oligolectic on different plant families: in the Southwest, species of *Diadasia* specialize on cacti and mallows, while *Diadasia* species elsewhere specialize on evening primroses or sunflowers.

"Monolectic" bees are more specialized still; they gather pollen from just a single species of flower. Because of the restricted range of their food sources, monolectic bees are particularly vulnerable to changes in their habitat.

SOCIAL NEST-BUILDING BEES

Social bees live in colonies, which are defined as having at least two adult females—there may be many more—who live in the same nest and share the work of preparing and provisioning it. Usually, one of them is the egg-laying queen and the others are workers. Bumble bees (genus *Bombus*) are the best-known social bees that are native to the United States. There are forty-seven species of bumble bees in North America, including six that are social parasites on the others. (Until recently, the parasitic species were in their own genus, *Psithyrus*.)

In addition to bumble bees, there are at least fifty other native bee species that nest socially. The most numerous are sweat bees, particularly those in the genera *Halictus* and *Lasioglossum*, which live colonially as an egg-laying female with female workers helping construct and supply the nest.

Nests of Social Bees

Bumble bees and social sweat bees have in common that they live in annual colonies founded in the spring by an individual queen after she wakes from hibernation. However, their nesting sites differ. The newly emerged bumble bee queen locates and nests within a dry cavity, perhaps in an abandoned mouse nest or under a tussock of grass (though some of these adaptable bee species will also nest in walls, discarded mattresses, or junked cars). The queen produces wax from glands in her body to make a few pot-like cells, lays her eggs, and then forages for nectar and pollen to feed her first brood of larvae. After a month or so the larvae pupate and emerge as worker bees. These worker bees do most of the work of constructing the nest and foraging, and once they are active the queen can use her energy to lay eggs.

Unlike the solitary bees, social bees pass quickly through the pre-pupal stage, pupate, and then become the next adult generation in the nest. Their entire development may take no longer than four or five weeks. During the summer the colony grows in size until late in the season, when a generation of new queens and males are produced, emerge, and mate. As fall arrives, most of the bees—including the old queen—die, leaving only the newly mated queens to overwinter and establish new colonies the following spring.

Unlike bumble bees—but like many of the solitary bees—social sweat bees nest in underground tunnels. In general, the emerging female digs a burrow in which she excavates brood cells, provisions them, lays her eggs, and rears her offspring, who then become her workers. Sometimes, however, two or more sister females will found

Though we commonly think of bees as living in hives, only a few species of bees are social. Bumble bees are probably the best-known social bees native to North America. In this photograph the worker bees are tending the waxy, ball-shaped brood cells, in which the white larvae can be seen. Edward S. Ross.

a communal nest in the spring, in which one lays eggs that the others tend. Since sweat bees nest in a way that is similar to that of the solitary ground-nesting species, they face the same threats and will be helped by the same conservation measures.

Foraging of Social Bees

Social bees are polylectic. To sustain the colony and feed the larvae through the spring and summer, they must gather food from flowering plants over an extended period. The best way to ensure these pollinators a steady food source is to plant a variety of plants that bloom at various times throughout the year. Many bumble bees have long tongues and prefer flowers that have deeper, more complex structures. Individual bees typically visit a single species of flower on any given foraging trip—the behavior called flower constancy—but they can adjust to the parade of plant communities that results from seasonal and habitat changes as long as suitable nesting sites are available.

PARASITIC BEES

About a quarter of bee species lay their eggs in the nests of other bee species in the same family as themselves. The parasitic bees of solitary bee species are called cuckoo bees (also known as cleptoparasites), and the parasitic bees of social bee species are called social parasites.

Among the solitary bee species, the cuckoo bee enters the host's nest to lay her eggs when the adult female is not present. The first act of the cuckoo bee larva after hatching is usually to kill the host bee's egg or larva. It then feeds on the host's food provisions, and will remain in the brood cell through larval and pupal stages before emerging as an adult. Among the social bees, the females of some species of social parasites kill the host queen, while the females of other species may live side-by-side with her. In either case, the duped workers raise the parasite's larvae as if they were their own. For all parasitic species the adults emerge later than those of their host species, since their eggs are laid only after the nests have been fully established.

FLIES

Flies, which are among the most frequent visitors to flowers, are often misidentified as bees, and for good reason. Flies can't sting, but sounding and looking like insects that can makes birds and other predators avoid them. Syrphid flies, for example, gain protection by mimicking the bold warning ("aposematic") coloration of bees and wasps.

To distinguish a fly from a bee, first examine its head. Most flower-visiting flies have short, fat, down-turned antennae, often with obvious bristles, while bees' antennae tend to be much longer and more uniform in thickness. Second, look at the wings. Flies have two—the scientific name for the order is Diptera, or "two wings"—and bees have four. Finally, look for bodily features that enable the insect to carry pollen on its legs or under its belly; female bees generally have such features and flies do not. Granted, some of these characteristics may be hard to discern on an insect feeding at a flower, but with practice, you can learn to see them at a glance.

Depending on the species, an adult fly's life span varies from a few hours to several weeks, and may even be as long as six months. Adult flies don't make nests, but rather lay their eggs close to (or within) a good supply of the larvae's preferred food, which varies greatly among fly species. The larval food of syrphid species, for example, includes detritus and aphids, while bee fly larvae are parasites in bee nests and small-headed fly larvae are internal parasites of spiders. The search for a suitable place to lay eggs requires energy, which many flies derive from flower nectar; in the process of feeding they act as pollinators.

A single fly transports less pollen than a single bee does, but flies, simply because of their numbers, are effective and important pollinators. They are especially important in northern regions and mountainous areas, where the temperatures are colder and the flowering periods shorter. These conditions are less favorable for bees, which require a lot of flower forage for an extended period when they are building and provisioning their nests and simultaneously providing for themselves. The female fly, however, since she does not construct a nest, needs only to provide for herself while finding first a mate and then a suitable place to lay her eggs.

Flower Flies

Flower flies—or hover flies—(family Syrphidae) are among the most colorful and conspicuous flies found around flowers. Many flower flies mimic bees and wasps in their coloring, an adaptation that enables them to confuse predators. For some species, this mimicry confers more than just protection while they are foraging. Flies in the genus *Volucella*, for example, make use of mimicry to enter the nests of bumble bees, where they lay their eggs. Their larvae feed on dead bees and other detritus in the nests.

The larvae of most other syrphid flies develop in less specialized conditions, but they still have particular food needs. Many flower flies lay their eggs on plants, where the larvae feed on other insects. (Look

Many pollinating flies resemble bees. Looking like a stinging insect gives some protection from predators, as in the case of this bumble-bee-mimicking syrphid (genus *Criorhina*). Flies differ from bees most obviously in the shape and size of their antennae and in the number of wings. Edward S. Ross.

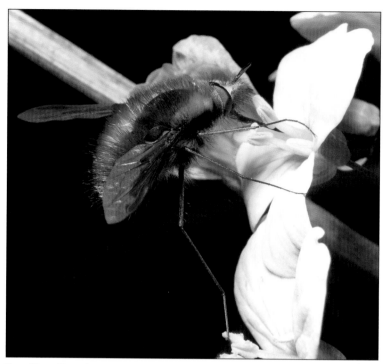

Bee flies (family Bombyliidae) are hairy flies with long proboscises that can reach nectar deep inside flowers. Edward S. Ross.

closely at a rose bush, and you may see a grub-like flower fly larva rearing up to consume an aphid.) Other species lay eggs on rotting wood, into which the larvae tunnel as they eat.

Bee Flies

The bee fly (family Bombyliidae), another important pollinator, is stout and hairy like a bumble bee; it can hover while feeding, using its prominent bristle-like proboscis to reach the nectar deep within flowers. Some species have banded or spotted wings that stick out sideways when the insect is at rest.

The larvae of most bee flies are parasites on other insect larvae, including those of butterflies, ground-nesting solitary bees, and wasps. A female bee fly will fly low over the prospective bee host's nesting site and scatter her eggs; some species drop them with great precision into the tiny nest entrance. When a larva hatches it crawls into a brood cell where it eats both the food supply and the host larva itself by sucking out the hemolymph (the insect equivalent of blood). Some bee flies lay eggs on flowers; when a larva hatches it attaches to a passing caterpillar or other immature insect and feeds on the host's hemolymph.

Other Fly Families

A third group of pollinator flies are the small-headed flies (family Acroceridae), named for their bulbous bodies and tiny heads. The larvae are internal parasites of spiders. The female lays her eggs on vegetation, often in masses. The newly hatched larvae are highly mobile and each will crawl until it finds a host spider—often a wolf spider in the family Lycosidae. The larva enters the spider's body through the soft cuticle of a leg joint and migrates to the abdomen where it matures, a process that results in the death of the host.

The Muscidae and Tachinidae are two other important pollinator fly families and, because they include the common housefly, are the ones with which most people are likely to have frequent contact. These medium- to large-sized flies are particularly hairy, which makes them effective pollinators. Muscid larvae live in dung or other debris and scavenge or prey on other dung inhabitants, while nearly all tachinid larvae are internal parasites of other insects, often caterpillars.

BUTTERFLIES AND MOTHS

Butterflies, possibly the best loved of all insects, are appreciated as benign creatures that add color, beauty, and grace to our gardens. Butterflies and moths belong to the same insect order, Lepidoptera, and while people can usually distinguish a butterfly from a moth, the two can sometimes be hard to tell apart.

In general, butterflies are brightly colored and fly by day, and moths are more likely to be colored in muted grays and browns and fly at night. But there are numerous exceptions: such moths as the burnets, foresters, and ctenuchids are day-flying and colorful, as are bee-mimic hawkmoths.

When they are at rest, you can see other distinguishing morphological and behavioral differences. Butterflies tend to hold their wings either partially open or closed vertically over their bodies, like the sails of tiny sailboats. Most moths, on the other hand, hold their wings flat, with the forewings covering the hindwings. Look closer and you'll notice that moths tend to be fatter and hairier than butterflies. Also, a butterfly antenna is a single filament with a clubbed tip (which on many skippers is bent or hooked), whereas a moth antenna may be broad and feathery, or a single filament that tapers to a point.

Feeding Habits

A butterfly or moth begins life as an egg laid on or near its particular host plant species. Each hatches as a tiny, soft-bodied caterpillar, eating and growing until it transforms into a pupa, or chrysalis, the mummy-like quiescent stage between larva and adult. "Chrysalis" is the name of both a stage in development and the encasing at this stage, during which the structure of the insect is being reorganized. Many moths also spin an additional layer of protection; from their silk glands they make a cocoon in which they complete the metamorphosis into sexually active, winged adults.

Caterpillars spend most of their time eating, and because they are particular about what they eat, the adult female must lay her eggs on or very near the appropriate food source lest her offspring starve. Some species are so selective in their food requirements that the insect will not survive without proximity to the plant, and many species that rely on a single particular food source are threatened when the plant population is threatened. The larvae of the endangered Karner blue butterfly (*Lycaeides melissa samuelis*), for example, feed only on the wild lupine (*Lupinus perennis*), a member of the pea family, and the habitat supporting the wild lupine—in the upper Midwest, eastern New York, and New Hampshire—is now in drastic decline, thus jeopardizing the survival of the butterfly.

Although we seldom see them because they are mostly nocturnal, moths such as this noctuid moth are significant pollinators of many plants. Edward S. Ross.

Nectar from flowers and sugar from running sap or overripe fruit provide most, but not all, of the nutrition that males of many butterfly and moth species need. They will also sip at muddy puddles or damp earth for the mineral salts; and they feed at animal scat, bird droppings, or animal carcasses to get the amino acids and other vital nutrients they need to generate spermatophores, the packets of sperm and nutrients that are transferred to the female during mating.

Surviving Winter

Different species of butterflies use different strategies to survive the winter or other extended periods of inclement weather. Most species pass the winter in protected surroundings—like leaf litter or dense vegetation—as eggs, caterpillars, or pupae. A few, such as those in the genera *Nymphalis* (mourning cloaks and tortoiseshells), and *Polygonia* (anglewings), overwinter as hardy adults. In natural conditions, these butterflies find shelter from predators and the cold and wet in a cave or tree cavity, under leaf litter, or among evergreen vegetation, but they will also seek winter refuge in such places as sheds and barns, or even in a cool room in a house.

Migration is another way that butterflies avoid inclement weather. Monarch butterflies (*Danaus plexippus*) fly south to overwinter in a few patches of oyamel fir forest in the mountains of Michoacan, Mexico, and in tree groves in California. They return north the following spring, although the individuals that begin the journey are not the ones that finish it. The monarchs lay eggs on plants of milkweed (genus *Asclepias*) as they travel and die along the way, gradually spreading northward over two or three generations. The ones that migrate again in September find their way—using the sun to navigate and their circadian clocks to adjust for daily changes in the sun's position—back to the overwintering sites far to the south.

While the monarch's migration is complete and regular, many other butterfly species emigrate periodically in patterns that are less consistent. The painted lady (*Vanessa cardui*) and the cloudless sulfur (*Phoebis sennae*), for example, may fly north to take advantage of host plants and nectar sources that become available in spring and summer. When summer turns to fall, some of these butterflies' offspring shift south, perhaps traveling far enough to avoid being killed by freezing winter temperatures.

Like this tailed orange (*Eurema proterpia*), butterflies usually rest with their wings closed above their bodies. They drink nectar from flowers through their long, straw-like tongues. Edward S. Ross.

Beetles

There are more than 340,000 identified species of beetles worldwide—including nearly 30,000 species in North America alone. Beetles have been treated as everything from fashion accessories to religious symbols. In sixteenth-century Elizabethan England, the wing covers ("elytra") of brightly colored metallic beetles adorned ladies' ball gowns; in ancient Egypt a stone or faience beetle was used as a talisman and a symbol of resurrection. Many species of beetle, though, are small and dark and go almost unnoticed. In fact, within the huge number of beetle families, there is a great variety in body shape and size.

Flower-Visiting Beetles

Beetles (order Coleoptera) represent the greatest diversity of pollinators, and were among the earliest known. Fossil records suggest that beetles, along with flies, were probably the first insect pollinators of prehistoric angiosperm flowers in the late Jurassic era, around 150 million years ago. (Bees are relative newcomers as pollinators, having appeared in the fossil record only about 100 million years ago, during the Cretaceous period.) These ancient flowers were open, with many stamens and pistils. Since then, flowers have evolved and adapted to the growing range of pollinators. Though beetles appear not to have adapted to evolving flower shapes, they remain important pollinators, especially for such "primitive" flowers as magnolias.

Within the immense diversity of beetles, not all visit flowers, but there are several families of beetles that include regular flower visitors and are likely to be familiar to people in Canada and the United States. The adult soldier beetles (family Cantharidae) have long, almost rectangular bodies, and are often bright red and black (resembling military uniforms from pre-camouflage days) or yellow and black. Long-horned beetles (family Cerambycidae) are also large, with antennae that may equal or exceed their body length. Among the scarab beetles (family Scarabaeidae) are dung beetles and other drably colored species, as well as some of the world's most spectacular insects, such as the chafers, which may be metallic green with silver or gold markings. Another family with metallic coloration is Buprestidae, the metallic wood-boring beetles, whose rounded bodies taper to the rear. The soft-winged flower beetles (family Melyridae) are common on flowers. They are usually less than half an inch long and fuzzy; most are brown or black, although some have bright red or orange markings. Another group of small but abundant beetles are the pollen or flower beetles (family Nitidulidae); in the summer, you can see them in great numbers on flowers or decaying fruit, another source of sugars.

Life History

The life span of adult beetles varies widely from just a few days to several months, but most flower-visiting species are active among the flowers for four weeks or less. A substantial percentage of beetles that feed at flowers eat pollen, and some even chew on the flower itself; this form of beetle interaction is called mess and soil pollination. Despite the damage they can cause with their chewing and rummaging, a little pollen sticks to the beetles' bodies and gets transferred from anther to stigma. Because of the abundance of these insects, even that small amount of pollen adds up, making the beetles significant pollinators. In desert areas, the importance of beetles as pollinators is compounded by the emergence of adults in synchrony with the seasonal blooming of flowers, either in the spring or during the summer rainy period.

As with flies, the food requirements for their larvae determine where female beetles lay their eggs. Many beetles lay eggs on or within dying or weakened trees, where their grub-like larvae burrow beneath the bark or through the wood. Because this is not a good source of nutrition, these larvae may take several years to develop fully, often relying on symbiotic microbes in their guts to digest cellulose in the wood. Larvae of the long-horned beetles are generally found in such places, although some prefer to live on freshly dead branches and stems. The presence of tunneling beetle larvae, par-

Soldier beetles such as this *Chauliognathus omissus* (family Cantharidae) are frequent visitors to flowers, and also predators of aphids and other pest insects. They have long, narrow bodies with nearly parallel sides, and are often black with bold red or yellow markings. Edward S. Ross.

ticularly those of long-horned beetles and metallic wood-boring beetles, is important to wood-nesting bees such as leafcutter and mason bees, because the females construct their nests within the abandoned beetle tunnels. Thus, a lack of beetle larvae may limit local bee populations.

Other beetle larvae are highly mobile predators that will eat other invertebrates. Leaf litter provides habitat for predatory soldier beetle larvae; and loose bark, plant galls, termite nests, soil and litter are foraging grounds for larvae of soft-winged flower beetles.

4

Threats to Pollinators

Human beings have been endlessly shaping and modifying the earth since the dawn of humankind. Some Native Americans, for instance, burned grasslands year after year to keep the forests from encroaching and thus create favorable habitat for game they would hunt and plants and fruit they would harvest. Today, with the power that we possess to rapidly, profoundly, and permanently alter landscapes for agriculture, ranching, forestry, mining, and development, the effects of our actions on plants and other animals can be disastrous.

Modern agriculture has seen the conversion of large areas of diverse prairies and other habitat into monocultures that offer few foraging or nesting opportunities for pollinators. Wheat harvest in eastern Washington, courtesy of the U.S. Department of Agriculture.

The clearing of land for development is a major reason for the loss of pollinator habitat. Matthew Shepherd.

There are three main threats to pollinators: the loss and fragmentation of habitat, habitat degradation, and pesticide poisoning. For many at-risk pollinator insect populations, the threats are multiple. In the United States, the twenty-four Lepidoptera species listed under the federal Endangered Species Act confront not only loss of habitat and poisoning from pesticides but threats from non-native species and pollution as well (in addition to overcollecting, a challenge that most other species do not face).

These threats are all the result of human activity. Although the impacts of our actions can never be completely reversed, it is human action alone that can begin the process of restoring pollinators and the balance they bring to the health of the ecosystem.

HABITAT LOSS AND FRAGMENTATION

Both the outright destruction of habitat and the fragmentation of habitat into small, isolated patches threaten the diversity and abundance of native pollinators. In urban areas the loss of wild habitat is apparent, but the fragmentation of habitat in rural areas is no less a problem. Farming and ranching practices leave the landscape green, but covered in fields that hold few foraging or nesting resources and are often laden with pesticides. What little habitat is left—field margins, hedgerows, roadside banks, and the sides of ditches and creeks—is very important for pollinators, though it tends to be weedy and to host fewer of the native plant species that they require.

Along with agriculture, commercial and residential development rank as the most frequent causes of habitat loss. These developments often are situated on sites that have naturally high diversity, such as along rivers or near bays and estuaries. Urban development in the southeastern United States and in California has had particularly strong impacts on native insects because many cities were built in coastal areas that were home to unique species and habitats. A striking instance is San Francisco, which now covers almost entirely what was once one of the major coastal dune ecosystems in western North America. Three dune butterflies that were endemic to this region are now extinct: the Xerces blue (*Glaucopsyche xerces*) and pheres blue (*Icaricia icarioides pheres*), which were well enough known to be given common names, and one other, *Cercyonis sthenele sthenele*. Three other butterflies, the callippe silverspot (*Speyeria callippe callippe*), the San Bruno elfin (*Callophrys mossii bayensis*), and the mission blue (*Icaricia icarioides missionensis*), are now reduced to only a handful of colonies each on the San Francisco peninsula; San Bruno Mountain, the last remnant of the San Francisco hills ecosystem, is vital for their survival.

HABITAT DEGRADATION

The two major factors contributing to habitat degradation are the influx of invasive species and certain land-management practices. The introduction of exotic organisms, whether intentional or not, has affected native insects both directly and indirectly. Invasive non-native plant species destroy habitat by crowding out the native plants that

In many landscapes habitat has been fragmented by farming and development. The patches that remain in hedgerows, field margins, and ditch banks can be quite valuable for pollinators. Matthew Shepherd.

have evolved with native pollinators and replacing them with plants that offer inferior foraging and egg-laying opportunities.

Changes in land-management practices that have come about as a result of new technologies can be employed to good effect but often lead to degraded habitats, especially when used in pursuit of a "tidy" landscape. Modern mowers, and line trimmers in particular, can cut places that previously would have been left to grow, reducing both the floral and structural diversity of a grassland. Herbicides used in place of hand weeding can kill not just the target species but all the plants, including those that provide forage for pollinators.

Finally, the increasing use of off-road vehicles often leads to severe habitat damage at popular recreation sites, particularly in sandy or dune areas.

PESTICIDES

In the early 1970s the blueberry farmers of New Brunswick, Canada, experienced a sudden decline in harvests because of the disappearance of the native bumble bees, mason bees, and mining bees that pollinated their crops. The lack of bees, they learned later, was caused by the aerial spraying of fenitrothion onto adjacent woodlands to kill spruce budworm. The spraying was stopped but it took three years for bee populations to rebound and for fruit harvests to recover their pre-spraying levels. In the southwestern United States, beekeepers reported large kills of their honey bees after insecticides were applied to Bermuda grass grown for seed. The bees were apparently foraging for pollen on the grass flowers because there weren't enough other blooming plants in these areas, and in the process they collected insecticide, which killed them. In Washington state, the diazinon applied to control aphids on alfalfa also decimated foraging alkali bees, which are an important pollinator of alfalfa; the death of female bees led to a 95-percent drop in the number of underground bee larvae in three nearby nesting sites studied by one investigator.

Virtually all of the research on the effect of pesticides on bees focuses on honey bees because of their importance to agriculture. However, the use of managed populations of solitary bees as pollinators of some crops—in particular, alfalfa leafcutter (*Megachile rotundata*) and alkali bees (*Nomia melanderi*) for alfalfa—has provided opportunities to extend our understanding of the impact of pesticides on native bees. The incidents described above are just three well-documented poisonings out of the many thousands that have occurred. The documentation of the New Brunswick bee kill is unusual in that it relates to wild bees. Far more often the impacts of pesticides on managed pollinators are documented while the extent of the killing of wild bees goes unnoted.

One thing is clear: insecticides and herbicides are having a disastrous effect on both managed and wild bee populations. Millions of pounds of pesticides are applied to farms, fields, lawns, flower beds, and roadsides every year. Insecticides kill pollinators directly, while herbicides reduce the diversity and abundance of the flowering plants that pollinators feed upon. Many pesticides degrade slowly, remaining as a lingering toxic hazard to pollinators and other wildlife.

Despite the threat, pesticide use in North America has continued to grow. In California, for example, pesticide sales grew by an average of 12.4 million pounds per year between 1991 and 1998. In the United States, according to the Environmental Protection Agency, total pesticide use in 1998 and 1999 exceeded 1.2 billion pounds—more than 20 percent of the pesticides used worldwide. Herbicides accounted for the largest proportion of this usage, followed by insecticides and fungicides.

Pesticides are not just a problem on agricultural lands. Studies conducted by the U.S. Geologic Survey and some municipalities have detected higher concentrations of pesticides in streams in urban areas than in streams in agricultural areas. We should not be surprised by this: a recent study in the Puget Sound Basin found that more pounds of pesticides were applied per acre in urban neighborhoods than on agricultural fields.

Impacts of Pesticides

Foraging bees are poisoned by pesticides when they absorb the fast-acting toxins through their integument (the outer "skin" that forms their exoskeleton), drink toxin-tainted nectar, or gather pesticide-covered pollen or micro-encapsulated poisons. If they are foraging while the pesticides are being applied, the spray or dust covers them, killing significant numbers of bees in the field. If they are foraging on recently sprayed fields, they absorb toxins from the residues on plants, which kills them more slowly.

Smaller bees—the majority of our native bees—are more sensitive; they have a larger surface area relative to their body volume and so absorb doses that are relatively higher. Thus insecticide residues on plants remain toxic longer for smaller bees, and they are killed by lower concentrations of poisons (such as those resulting from spray drift). After a significant kill, beekeepers may find thousands of dead honey bees in and around each hive. One can only imagine the thousands of dead native bees that at the same time are scattered around the landscape out of sight.

Even less-than-lethal doses of pesticides can have substantial adverse effects. Bees that are exposed outside the nest may have trouble navigating their way back to the nest after foraging, or they may be unable to fly at all. Other symptoms include aggressive or agitated be-

Extensive use of pesticides is a major cause of pollinator declines. Insecticides directly kill pollinators and herbicides eliminate potential foraging plants. Courtesy of the U.S. Department of Agriculture.

havior, jerky or wobbly movements, or paralysis, all of which make foraging and nest building difficult. Sub-lethal doses can result from direct contact with pesticides or from toxins brought into the nest with nectar and pollen, and may impact egg laying in the nest as well as the next generation of bees.

Given the harm that pesticides inflict both directly and indirectly, as well as the weaknesses of the guidelines in protecting native pollinators, we unequivocally recommend against the use of pesticides.

Alternatives to Pesticides

There are many things you can do to eliminate or limit the need for pesticides. First, ensure that your plants are healthy. A plant that is growing vigorously, with minimal stress, can avoid or outgrow many disease and insect pest problems. It is preferable to choose plants appropriate to the conditions rather than to try to create artificial conditions to suit an exotic plant. A locally native plant will by nature grow better in your local conditions than a non-native plant.

Good soil is the foundation of a healthy garden. Providing soil amendments and adequate nutrients will benefit your plants. Conventional chemical-based and factory-manufactured fertilizers are not necessary; composts and natural fertilizers are very effective. Natural fertilizers tend to improve the soil not only by adding nutrients but by improving its structure and organic material content as well.

It is also important to recognize and work with naturally occurring controls against pests. A healthy and diverse pollinator garden has most of the necessary habitat elements to encourage native predators or parasites of pest insects, while pesticides often eliminate the natural enemies of common pest species and leave you with chronic problems. You should also avoid over-the-counter biological controls, as they can cause long-term ecological problems. For example, the wide-scale release of non-native ladybird beetles (commonly referred to as "ladybugs") is thought to be a key reason for the decline in native ladybird beetles. It is much better to encourage your own native insect controls than to introduce species that are not locally native.

In small areas, practices such as hand picking and crushing insects or spraying a stream of soapy water to dislodge aphids from plants may be practical and effective. You can also limit the spread of disease by practicing good sanitation—basically, removing diseased leaves and other material from the area. However, this may not be practical in large areas, where managers may want to implement the approach known as integrated pest management as an alternative to pesticides alone.

If You Really Must Use Pesticides

If you feel you have to use pesticides, you certainly want to minimize the damage that you do to pollinators that benefit your plants, and to other insects that are the natural enemies of many pest insects. It is important that you apply pesticides when pollinators are not active, or during those seasons when there are no blooms present on the plants. Finally, avoid spraying bee nesting areas, caterpillar host plants, and places where there are fly and beetle larvae.

The application of pesticides is greatest in domestic yards and gardens; as noted above, more pounds of pesticides are applied per acre in urban areas than on agricultural lands. Home gardeners can buy any available product and use it without training or supervision, with the result that chemicals are often applied in back yards in quantities far greater than those recommended by the manufacturer.

Pesticides on larger, commercially managed landscapes have their own problems. They may be applied in a variety of ways, from backpack sprayers to aerial application. Pesticide drift from aerial spraying onto adjacent crops or wildflowers may kill 80 percent of foraging bees close to the source, but drift can continue to be dangerous for a mile and a half or further. Not only is aerial application an inefficient and destructive method, it is also an expensive one.

While there are written guidelines to protect pollinating insects during the application of pesticides, these have been developed to protect honey bee hives and the few other bee species that are managed for pollination. They provide little protection for wild bees, be-

A common sight in agricultural areas, aerial spraying of pesticides results in the killing of non-target species, both pollinator insects and the native plants on which they forage. Courtesy of the U.S. Department of Agriculture.

cause there are no restrictions on pesticide use to protect pollinators when managed bees are not active, despite the fact that wild bees may be foraging on field margins or nearby wildlands. Moreover, unless people adhere to them, the guidelines offer no protection for pollinators at all. For example, spraying for mosquito abatement by local county and city governments should be done at night, but when "public health" programs get behind schedule, agencies don't necessarily follow their own guidelines. Daylight spraying can devastate local bee populations.

Pesticides will always have an impact on pollinators, whether it's because the poisons kill the bees directly in the fields or because they linger on foraging plants. The best decision is not to use pesticides at all, but if you must, consider the likely impacts on pollinators and do everything you can to minimize them.

OTHER POTENTIAL THREATS

Over the past century, non-native insects have been released in order to control—as predators, parasites, or herbivores—pest insects and non-native invasive plants. This biological control is often touted as a safe alternative to chemicals, and is now frequently applied. However, increasing evidence suggests that the negative impacts of such releases on non-target, native species can be significant.

Studies in Illinois have demonstrated that ladybird beetles (family Coccinellidae) introduced to control aphids on crops also feed upon early instars of monarch butterflies. Similarly, in Hawaii, a recent study found that 83 percent of parasitoids found in native moths were species that had originally been introduced for biological control of pest species, and that now parasitize a wide range of host species.

Indirectly, insects released for the purpose of controlling non-native invasive plants can affect native pollinators by reducing food availability. For example, two European weevil species released in North America to control non-native thistles now adversely impact native thistles, reducing an important nectar source for a range of pollinator insects.

Overcollecting may be yet another important threat, not to most populations of pollinator insects but to those whose populations are imperiled. Also, lights along streets and highways are apparently responsible for losses of nocturnal insects, particularly large moths. Finally, although we cannot specify the precise effects of climate change at this time, the phenomenon of global warming could lead to the loss of endemic insects that have specific, narrow habitat requirements. A changing climate may be especially detrimental to species that cannot disperse, such as the Uncompahgre fritillary (*Boloria improba acrocnema*), which is found only on high mountain slopes in southern Colorado.

5

Actions to Help Pollinators

The best way to attract and support healthy pollinator populations is to ensure a rich, diverse plant community; conversely, an abundance and diversity of insect pollinators will yield a fertile and productive landscape. By protecting existing habitat, restoring degraded areas, and creating new foraging and nesting sites, we can provide for the needs of pollinators. Whether you are working in a small yard or on a large expanse of land, the conditions that you will want to create all have these features:

◆ **A diversity of native plants whose blooming times overlap to provide flowers for foraging throughout the seasons.** In any location, native flowers, which are adapted to local soils and climates, are the best source of nectar and pollen for native pollinators. In residential yards and gardens, heirloom plant varieties may also be beneficial.

◆ **Nesting and egg-laying sites, with appropriate nesting materials.** Bees require sites in the ground or woody vegetation as well as nesting materials, and butterflies need appropriate host plants for their caterpillars. The egg-laying needs of flies and beetles are not easily defined, but are provided by a diverse, pesticide-free habitat.

◆ **Sheltered, undisturbed places for hibernation and overwintering.** Many insects live for over a year, but they are active adults for only the last few days or weeks of their lives. Pollinators require secure places during the months when they are dormant pupae or hibernating adults.

◆ **A landscape free of poisonous chemicals.** The use of pesticides in gardens, on farms, and in managed landscapes is a major threat to pollinators. Insecticides kill and injure pollinator insects directly, while herbicides harm them by damaging the plants that offer them foraging and egg-laying opportunities. Pesticides should be kept away from pollinator habitat.

For pollinators to thrive, your habitat should offer nesting and overwintering sites as well as a diversity of native plants, and should be free of pesticides. Flower-rich sunny meadows fringed with trees can provide excellent habitat for pollinators. Mace Vaughan.

Studies done in Western Europe show that the habitats that support the most diverse bee populations are old grasslands, heathlands, and hedgerows, all of which contain a diversity of flowers, dead wood, and areas of bare soil for nesting sites, as well as mud, resin, and other nest-building materials. Shady places, particularly conifer forests, provide fewer floral resources and are the least used by bees.

Many bees and other pollinators can adapt to patchy, human-influenced landscapes because in natural conditions their foraging plants and nest sites are likely to have patchy distributions. Does this mean we should not be concerned because pollinators can adapt to whatever we do? Sadly, no. Several butterfly species are known to have gone extinct in the United States due to human activities, and a large number of other pollinators, including many of Hawaii's sixty-two native bee species, are known to be vulnerable. Although many pollinating insects can adapt to changing conditions and often rebound from the effects of natural changes in their environment—including fires, floods, droughts, and windstorms—we cannot protect a diversity of pollinators without a critical mass of diverse habitats, and that critical mass is being lost in many landscapes.

Not only is there less natural habitat, but the land that surrounds it is often inhospitable to pollinators because it lacks food plants or nesting sites. In rural areas, the fields created by large-scale agriculture are too big for some bee species to cross to reach forage or nests; and tilling can destroy shallow bee nests. The crops grown on many farms are wind-pollinated members of the grass family (wheat, corn, rice, grass, barley, oats, etc.) and have little or no value as bee forage, while those crops that do offer nectar and pollen usually provide them only in a brief burst.

In urban areas, landscapes around developments tend to be dominated by easy-to-maintain lawns and shrubs chosen for their colorful foliage rather than for their flowers. When there are flowers, often they are non-native plants and provide little or no food value for native pollinators.

Protecting and Restoring Habitat

The first step toward conserving pollinator diversity is to protect existing habitat. This includes the smaller, more marginal patches that offer just one or two of the resources pollinators need, as well as larger and more visible areas. While smaller areas usually lack a diversity of native plants, they do have benefits for pollinators, especially in contrast to monocultured—and sometimes poison-laden—agricultural lands. Indeed, research in Europe has shown the value that land on the margins of farms has for pollinators. In Germany the loss of hedgerows, highway verges, and similar landscape features has been associated with declines in pollinator insects, while in Poland these habitat patches have been retained, and so have the rich and diverse pollinator fauna that depend upon them.

A dead tree in a hedgerow or a patch of bare soil on a roadside bank or railroad embankment can be a bee nesting site. Flowers growing along a roadside verge, in a field margin, on a creek bank, in a garden border, or in an undeveloped space offer nectar for adults or host plants for caterpillars. In short, it is important to protect the patchwork of habitat fragments that host flowers and nesting sites. Human artifacts can also offer unintended benefits. Fences, barns, and other structures may provide nesting sites for wood-nesting bees. Within agricultural and urban landscapes there are many such possibilities, which taken together provide a mosaic of valuable pollinator habitats. But it is important for these discrete patches to be located close to each other, as many native bees do not travel more than a quarter of a mile.

There is still excellent habitat of significant size that can support robust and diverse pollinator populations. The Pinnacles National Monument in California, with more than four hundred species of bees, is one such place. The astonishing bee diversity at Pinnacles makes it a site of national importance, but there are many smaller sites that, although they may have fewer bees, are of local or regional significance. The creation of new habitat and the restoration of marginal

In agricultural areas the hedgerows and banks associated with roads and field margins provide important habitat and should be protected. This sun-dappled lane, with its flowers, trees, and bare ground, offers both foraging and nesting opportunities. Matthew Shepherd.

habitat will not replace the complex ecosystems that have developed over centuries. And the work we do to create and restore habitat will succeed only if we also protect these areas of high diversity, for they provide refugia from which the re-colonization of surrounding lands may be possible.

We can also improve on present conditions if we consciously plan and create habitat patches—the bigger the better—in urban, suburban, and rural areas. We can plant a diversity and abundance of nectar- and pollen-laden native plants, we can provide nesting habitat, and we can choose not to use pesticides. The pollinators will come, and with them, the fruits, flowers, and vegetables that we enjoy.

Taking Political Action

This handbook emphasizes what you as an individual can do to protect and strengthen pollinator populations by guiding you through the steps necessary in your back yard, school grounds, or natural area to manage or enhance pollinator habitat. However, if we are going to protect pollinators for the long term, we must consider these species and their ecological role in a larger context, and we must enact policies and procedures that protect them on a larger scale.

In 1998 a group of pollination scientists developed recommendations for conserving pollinators. Their findings, published in the journal *Conservation Biology* and endorsed by numerous conservation organizations and professional societies, recommended that more attention be given to invertebrate taxonomy, monitoring, and re-introduction as part of habitat management and restoration plans. The scientists underscored the necessity for research to assess the large-

In Britain, where they are protected by legislation, hedgerows and verges have been retained in both agricultural and urban landscapes. Such features provide sanctuary to pollinators and other wildlife. Matthew Shepherd.

ly unquantified effects of pesticides, herbicides, and habitat fragmentation on wild pollinator populations. They urged that floral reserves along migration corridors of threatened migratory pollinators be identified and protected, and they emphasized the importance of education and training to ensure that the general public, law makers, and resource managers understand the importance of pollinators and the ecosystem services they provide.

All of these recommendations were based on the premise that if we are going to protect any species we must know where it is found, understand its biological needs, and preserve its habitat. Some insects require only small areas to thrive; thus, even backyard gardens and patches of urban greenspace are useful. Some good pollinator habitat may lie a little farther afield, in parks and open spaces, railroad and highway verges, and power-line rights of way. Often, these areas contain wildflowers and form valuable wildlife corridors between patches of conserved vegetation.

Conservationists have labored over many years to have large swaths of land set aside as reserves, wilderness, national parks, and conservation easements. These areas benefit many species of plants and animals and also have important long-term benefits to pollinator diversity. In addition, the formal listing of species as threatened or endangered under the Endangered Species Act has been an extremely effective tool for protecting endangered butterflies, even if other groups of pollinators have not benefited. This law mandates that any land development requiring a federal or state permit must protect endangered species that may be impacted, including listed pollinators.

As a citizen, there are many ways you can affect policy. Work with your local conservation groups to protect and expand open space areas, wildlife refuges, and wilderness areas. Find out who manages the plants and animals in your neighborhood or nearby open areas, and encourage them to include pollinators in their management plans. Controlled burns, for example, though they are an important tool for maintaining open grassland habitat, must be timed and managed with pollinators in mind lest they decimate their populations. Work with local park managers to minimize the use of pesticides. Contact your local mosquito-abatement district to learn what it is doing to minimize the impact on pollinators.

You also can help educate your community about the importance of pollinators. You can teach teachers, students, friends, neighbors, colleagues—and anyone else who will listen—about pollination. Help your elected officials understand the crucial role that pollinators play in urban yards and gardens. Watch for development proposals that might affect a hedgerow or flowering field margin, and then talk to the city planners about protecting it. Contact the agencies responsible for highway margins and advocate that maintenance crews cut only bushes and higher vegetation, and only where public safety demands it. Suggest that native plants and seeds be used in public areas. These might seem like small steps to address a big problem, but together the actions of individual citizens in their local parks, neighborhoods, and back yards can have a significant impact. Everything you do will make a difference.

6

Planning Your Pollinator Habitat

Pollinator conservation can be done on any scale and adapted to any situation. Whether you are a homeowner working in your own garden, a land manager for a city park, a farmer with field margins, or a steward for a nature preserve, the pollinators' four basic requirements are the same: they need foraging opportunities, egg-laying and nesting sites, hibernation and overwintering sites, and a habitat free of pesticides. The conservation actions necessary to create pollinator habitat are easy to implement and require little technical knowledge or special equipment.

Although the principles for establishing pollinator habitat are the same regardless of where you are working, variations in the size, ecology, and management goals of different sites mean that each has its own particular considerations. In this chapter you will find guidance on planning a pollinator conservation project as well as ideas to help you enhance pollinator habitat at a range of scales and locations.

Planning for a Successful Project

Whether you are working to create habitat on a golf course, in a natural area, or in your own back yard, planning is an important first step. In your back yard, this may simply involve deciding which flowers to plant and where to create nesting sites. (For more on residential yards and gardens, see page 63.) Other lands may require significantly more planning because of factors such as size, public use, or the cost of management. You will have to balance the details of pollinator conservation with the other goals and uses of the site. If your site protects migratory birds, for example, providing for pollinator insects may be a secondary concern. You will also want to think about which specific areas are best suited for restoration or creation of pollinator habitat; how to ensure easy maintenance of and access to the site; how to plan a budget and raise funds; and how to involve people who need or want to be involved in the project, which may mean educating them about the benefits of pollinators.

The Site

In any project, finding the right location will probably involve a compromise between the ideal and the practical. You will need to consider the existing conditions: the slope and aspect of the site, the location of trees, the size of the area you are working in, and its current uses. In any of these places, there may be practical considerations, such as ways of getting vehicles and irrigation equipment to the site for maintenance tasks.

Begin by studying the site so that you know what it offers in the way of plant communities, other wildlife, and water. If there are areas with good foraging plants or potential nesting sites, focus your efforts on improving or enlarging them. Then look at the land between these areas; if it has little habitat value, consider adding patches of flowering plants or nesting and egg-laying sites to create stepping stones— habitat corridors—between the principal pollinator areas.

If this land is important for other wildlife, of course you will not want to disturb or cut it in order to create a flower-rich foraging area for bees, and it may in any case be valuable for pollinators in other ways. Woodland margins that are too shady to be home to forage flowers may contain beetle-riddled snags and logs in which bees can nest or on which syrphid flies can lay eggs. Similarly, wetlands may not suit ground-nesting bees, but may well contain flowers for foraging and probably twigs or reed stems that offer nesting sites for wood-nesting bees.

When you are identifying locations for new pollinator habitat, select areas that are sunny and warm. In general, nests for wood-nesting bees should face southeast or east, and those for ground-nesting bees should face south and be well drained. For foraging habitat, south-facing areas that are sheltered from the wind are usually warmer, which is preferable for both bees and butterflies. In the arid South-west or other areas with extreme summer heat, southeast- or east-facing sites might be preferred for foraging, as microhabitats that face due south are sometimes too hot and dry. Trees have both advantages and disadvantages: alive, they act as windbreaks to help warm a site and they can be a source of abundant nectar and pollen, though they may create too much shade. Dead, they provide nesting sites for soli-tary bees and places to lay eggs for some flies and beetles.

The planning considerations for a large natural site may be very different from those for a utility easement or a backyard garden, but all of these areas can be a component of the habitat mosaic that supports pollinators in our increasingly human-altered landscapes. Edward S. Ross.

As far as configuration, habitat patches that are bigger, rounder, and closer to other patches will generally be better than those that are smaller, of uneven shapes, and more isolated from one another. Siting conservation areas away from where people may be playing sports, biking, or mowing will be less disruptive to the insects.

Site Maintenance

During the project's planning stages, consider its long-term management in order to minimize the effort needed for future maintenance. For example, you will want to choose plants that are appropriate for the growing conditions and that require minimal care. You can find the best information regarding appropriate native plant materials from local nurseries, native plant societies, and bookstores. If you anticipate needing resources such as volunteers, equipment, or money, you will want to plan in advance in order to avoid the demoralizing experience of spending time and energy on a project that fails for lack of follow through.

The Budget

Soon after you determine to launch a pollinator-habitat conservation project, you will want to think about the costs both of getting it going and of maintaining it over time. Your biggest single expenses will be plant material and labor. Planting from seed is much cheaper than using container-grown plants (although the latter may be preferable for other reasons). To reduce your labor costs, you may want to approach landscaping companies and nurseries for in-kind donations. And for many projects, volunteers can do much of the work.

There are also grants available to support projects for habitat creation and protection, particularly to nonprofit organizations and educational institutions, or on sites where there is a community benefit or where educational activities can be included. Your county extension service, your local library, and the internet can supply information on private foundations, corporations, federal and state agencies, city governments, and environmental organizations that

When the habitat is in a public place or there is community involvement, many opportunities exist for educational events or interpretation, like this panel at the Arizona Sonora Desert Museum. Stephen L. Buchmann.

support such projects. Agencies may also offer grants to support management of at-risk species. Farms in the United States may be eligible for aid under the Conservation Reserve Program, which targets watershed protection projects, but includes creating wildlife habitat as one potential use for Program land. In addition, the Conservation Reserve Enhancement Program—a component of the Conservation Reserve Program that operates in some areas of the United States—offers larger grants for the establishment of wildlife habitat. A third federal program that might assist with funding for pollinator improvements is the Wildlife Habitat Incentives Program, which is available to private landowners.

Planning for Public Sites

When you are planning a project for a public site, it is important to involve local people and other interested parties early in the process so they will be committed to the project and there will be fewer obstacles later. Getting people involved early may require that you seek them out rather than wait for them to come to you. Volunteers may include people from the neighborhood, gardeners and farmers, or members of local environmental organizations. Boy Scout and Girl Scout groups are often interested in doing conservation and habitat-maintenance work, for which the scouts may earn merit badges. Your county extension service can provide advice on plant suppliers.

During the planning stage you will also want to identify and co-ordinate with the various people and departments responsible for maintenance of the grounds. Schools, for example, may have such re-sponsibilities divided between multiple departments, each of which may have different expectations or requirements. You don't want to plant flowers one weekend only to discover that the landscape crew has instructions to mow that area the following week. Some school districts strictly divide responsibility according to the type of vege-tation, and you may find that the maintenance crew has to cut any grass that is planted, whether it is in your habitat area or not, or that you are responsible for the upkeep of any flowers you plant.

Since publicly accessible land has multiple uses, you will want to consider the activities and interests of the various users. Horseback riders, mountain bikers, or hikers, for example, can damage habitat. So can golfers searching for stray balls. Neighbors may be curious about what you are doing in their park. Take the initiative to talk to other area users early on about the project, get them involved if they're interested, and answer any questions or concerns they might have. They may not appreciate the grass not being mown, but if you explain how interesting the pollinator project will be for their children—and how beneficial for their tomato plants—you may win converts.

You might need to take an active role in educating people, such as providing written information materials, installing an interpreta-tive sign near the habitat, or organizing simple outreach activities. An article in your neighborhood newspaper can stir up interest. Invite a botanist, a biologist, or an entomologist from a local college or high school to offer guided walks. Organize a "pollinator-dependent" potluck party; it's a great way for neighbors to get together. Many peo-ple like to be involved in their community and, once they know about your project, may want to participate.

Residential Yards and Gardens

A typical yard fulfills many purposes—it's an attractive setting for a house, a place to relax on a summer afternoon, a play area for children, a setting for social gatherings. Providing for pollinators is compatible with all of these uses. Flower beds can be designed and planted with a range of native flowers and heirloom varieties that provide nectar and pollen for bees, or are the preferred caterpillar host plants for butterflies. Avoid using pesticides, and include some patches of bare ground and some bee nesting blocks—painted or decorated any way you like. In larger gardens, there may be space for a flowery meadow, a small orchard, or a beetle-riddled snag.

Remember too, that a little creative thinking and compromise can result in the greatest benefits all around. For example, if having a tidy,

Gardens, even small ones, can provide good habitat. Native and non-native plants offer food for pollinators and create an attractive place for people. Matthew Shepherd.

mowed lawn is important to you, consider setting your mower higher to allow for a little extra length, and letting the clover or violets grow—or planting them. They will make a much richer habitat for pollinator insects, and a more interesting lawn for you.

If you are working on a community garden, you probably already appreciate how essential pollinators are for your fruits and vegetables. Nesting blocks erected throughout the garden and wildflowers grown along the margins between plots will help support bee populations, as will keeping the garden free of pesticides. If there is an unused garden plot, it could become a site for ground-nesting bees. Cooperatively managed, it will benefit every gardener.

In urban and suburban areas there are many greenspaces that can be managed to provide pollinator habitat, even if only temporarily. The grass and flowers have been allowed to grow on this vacant development site, providing foraging and egg-laying sites for many different bees and butterflies. Matthew Shepherd.

School Yards

Like residential yards and gardens, school grounds offer many opportunities for creating enhanced pollinator habitats. If your school already has an appropriate wildlife area, it is easy to integrate the needs of pollinators, but you can also provide foraging and nesting habitat by planting flower beds next to the buildings and along walkways, or by transforming the margins of sports fields into habitat corridors, with wildflowers planted adjacent to hedgerows and nesting sites in sunny corners. Some school users might complain if the grounds appear untidy, but there are many low-growing flowering plants that can survive below the maximum cutting height of a mower and provide good forage for pollinators.

Many of these enhancements—nesting sites and foraging areas—will also create an outdoor laboratory that can be the source of stimulating biology and botany lessons and art classes. In addition to these direct benefits, the planning and implementing of a pollinator habitat project that involves students, parents, local businesses, or other volunteers can help to strengthen ties between the school and the community.

Urban Greenspaces

The greenspaces scattered through urban and suburban areas vary from river corridors and urban trails to carefully manicured city parks. Nature parks are clearly suitable as pollinator habitat. City parks and sports fields, by contrast, have diverse and perhaps specialized purposes; though these places may seem less hospitable to pollinator conservation efforts, habitat can often be created on marginal land interspersed among the other uses. Indeed, all urban greenspaces offer potential for pollinators, and can become important links in a chain of wildlife habitat through developed land.

Where natural areas have been retained, conservation efforts should focus on locating and protecting existing nesting sites and foraging areas, which likely already have pollinator populations that will benefit immediately from your efforts. If necessary, enrich the plant communities with locally native flowers and create additional nesting sites. Where space allows, expand these areas, because larger habitat patches are more likely to contain the combination of nesting, egg-laying, and foraging resources that support healthy pollinator populations.

Although almost any site can be managed for pollinators, the most suitable ones will be sunny, sheltered areas with flowers, older trees, and some bare ground. These might include grassy areas on the southern edge of woodlands, hedgerows, and south-facing earthen banks. Aim to develop a chain of habitat. A collection of isolated island-like patches will help pollinators, but if you can create corridors of improved habitat, the benefits increase greatly.

Many parks have—in addition to informal areas—established flower beds and borders that can be planted with beautiful native and heirloom flowers that will benefit bees, butterflies, and other pollinators.

GOLF COURSES

Golf courses are commonly perceived to be artificial, chemically maintained landscapes; the reality can be quite different, however, and many courses support a wide variety of wildlife. Indeed, golf courses that are surrounded by development or agriculture often contain the best habitats around. Out-of-play areas often exceed the playing area, sometimes several-fold, and can be suitable for pollinators because they are usually free of directly applied pesticides. Golf courses offer two major opportunities for pollinator conservation: the protection of existing natural vegetation and nesting sites, and the creation of new habitats in which pollinator communities can thrive.

The priorities and opportunities on a golf course are essentially the same as those for urban greenspaces. First, try to protect, enhance, and expand existing natural sites in out-of-play areas; then work to

Surrounding the greens, tees, and fairways of golf courses are many acres of out-of-play land. These offer great potential for wildlife, either through protection of existing habitat or creation of new habitat. Matthew Shepherd.

develop interlinking habitat patches in between. In addition, flower beds near buildings and tees can be planted with showy native flowers and heirloom varieties.

BUSINESS CAMPUSES

The opportunities for pollinator conservation on business campuses are very similar to those in such other carefully managed landscapes as city parks or golf courses. Many campuses contain extensive acreage of open land, either as permanent greenspace in which employees can exercise or relax, or as future expansion sites. The first priority is to protect the existing natural landscape features. In larger campuses, colorful flowering meadows and areas of prairie-like grassland can be created. Where there is not much space, or close to buildings where

Native plants would be preferable to these pansies, which, like many hybridized flowers are colorful but may offer little or no nectar or pollen to pollinators. Matthew Shepherd.

long grass may seem untidy and unprofessional, you can plant flower beds or create short swards rich in low-growing flowers that are easily maintained by setting the mower at its highest cutting height. As in any pollinator habitat, pesticides should be avoided.

Pollinators are not the only ones to benefit from these improvements. Employees will enjoy the wonderful colors, sounds, and smells. Native plants require less intensive management and less water, which reduces maintenance costs. And, of course, a conservation project can provide good publicity for a company, and the chance to develop more positive partnerships with the community.

HIGHWAY AND RAILROAD VERGES

In an increasingly modified and fragmented landscape, the verges along roads and railroads can offer important habitat for pollinators and wildlife. In urban areas, roadside vegetation serves as wildlife corridors connecting areas of habitat, or as significant patches of habitat in their own right. The same is true in farmland, where most ground is under the plow. For example, in some Midwestern states, remnants of prairie vegetation survive on roadsides, providing refuge for several less common species of butterflies. Moreover, one study showed that fewer butterflies were killed by traffic in the area of these remnants because the butterflies tended to stay sipping nectar supplied by the flower-rich vegetation rather than flying away to look elsewhere for forage.

Where species-rich grassland exists along highways and railroads, it's important to plan not only so that the flowers have time to bloom, but also so that long grass can remain for butterfly egg laying or bumble bee nests; this may mean cutting in the late fall or winter, and only every other year. Wherever possible, you can enrich foraging habitat with native plants, being careful to select species that will not become weeds in adjacent fields. Again, keep in mind that insecticides should not be used and that herbicides aimed at broad-leafed plants will kill

In densely developed districts, the patches of vegetation between roads at intersections can contribute to pollinator conservation as part of a more comprehensive effort. Mace Vaughan.

most of the plants that pollinators depend upon for egg laying and foraging.

Road and railroad verges often have exposed soil and rock on embankments and road cuts, which may be suitable for ground-nesting bees. If possible, keep or create bare ground for them, particularly on south-facing, well-drained slopes. In addition, snags and fallen logs left in hedgerows and at the edges of woods provide nest sites for wood-nesting bees.

Utility Easements

Utility easements contain a significant acreage of valuable habitat for pollinators because power line easements are mostly scrub or grassland, where tall trees cannot be allowed to grow. In many places, maintaining the current management will probably sustain these open conditions. As with road verges, the cutting of grass and shrubs should be planned to ensure that late-flowering plants—such as goldenrod, a very important late-season nectar source in those regions where it grows—are allowed to bloom and that uncut areas are left for pollinators to pupate and overwinter. Dividing an area into plots and cutting them on a three- or four-year rotation will maintain a suitable diversity of conditions. Some easements are increasingly important for wildlife in a degraded landscape, and may, for example, be a refuge for rare butterflies. In situations like this, there may be times when specific management efforts are required to maintain optimum conditions and a biologist should be consulted. As with other pollinator habitat, the use of pesticides should be avoided.

Farms

Farmers can do a lot to encourage native bees and other insect pollinators and, since many crop species need pollinators, the benefits are mutual. Marginal lands, such as field edges, hedgerows, sub-irrigated areas, and drainage ditches, offer both nesting and foraging sites. Areas

Kept clear of trees for safety reasons, utility easements are well suited for pollinator habitat, which can be enhanced by adding a nesting block as shown here. Matthew Shepherd.

left untilled, such as woodlots, conservation areas, utility easements, and farm roads, can support native bees. All of these places can be especially valuable if they are enhanced with bee foraging plants—to create "bee pasture"—but only if they are kept free of pesticide drift.

Ground-nesting bees seldom nest in rich soils, so the poorest soils will provide fine sites. These bee areas do not have to be large; planting hedgerows of shrubs and perennials, for example, can produce excellent bee habitat and will help to provide corridors across agricultural landscapes. When managed with pollinators in mind, farmlands can become important havens for these vital insects. And farmers growing insect-pollinated crops have a long-term economic and ecological interest in nurturing healthy pollinator populations.

Wild Areas

Wild areas are often a mosaic of distinct habitats—including oak savannah, scrublands, and herb-rich grasslands—in which pollinators thrive. Additionally, areas of transition, such as woodland or forest edges, often contain mature trees, snags, and fallen logs that provide nest sites, as well as shrubs and other small plants that offer foraging opportunities.

Managing for pollinators will not generally require a major overhaul of existing wildlife management plans and goals. However, pollinator conservation in wild—or partially wild—areas, such as nature preserves, state parks, and national parks and monuments, does require a different approach from many of those previously discussed because of both the size of the sites and the diversity of management goals. Typically, managers of natural areas focus on maintaining their

Wild areas such as this oak prairie offer excellent foraging opportunities for a wide variety of pollinator insects. Matthew Shepherd.

site's ecological integrity, often measured by its relative biodiversity. In other instances, site goals may be directed at the conservation or restoration of individual species or groups of species (e.g., waterfowl conservation in National Wildlife Refuge wetlands), and pollinators may not be a focus in the management of these areas.

Three of the major land-management issues affecting pollinators are grazing, fire management, and control of invasive species. Many areas managed for wildlife are grazed and trampled by livestock. This can be highly damaging, leading to a loss in both the floral and structural diversity of the habitat because the sward height is uniformly low, forage flowers or host plants are eaten, and the disturbance of fragile areas allows invasive weeds to become established.

Fire is a valuable technique for prairie management, but if pollinators are not considered in the management plan—especially butterflies and twig-nesting bees—their populations can be devastated. Although adult pollinator insects are mobile and some may be able to avoid fire, their eggs, larvae, and pupae cannot. In a well-designed fire-management plan that considers all of the area's species, managers will burn only a small percentage of the site in any given year. At some sites, an extended rotation of ten years or more may be appropriate. Unburned habitat will serve as a source for re-colonization of insects after the fire.

Invasive species must be controlled—and indeed, such control will generally be beneficial to pollinators—but land managers should be cautious and measured in their methods; using broad-spectrum herbicides to control weeds and maintain and restore native plant communities can indirectly harm pollinators by removing either caterpillar host plants or foraging flowers that provide pollen and nectar for existing populations.

Some management practices may unnecessarily harm pollinator populations, but if managers recognize the important ecosystem function of pollination, its role in plant propagation, and the biodiversity inherent in a strong community of pollinator insects, they will more readily consider the needs of these organisms in their decisions.

7

Providing Foraging Habitat

The foraging needs of a diversity of pollinators will be met with a diversity of plants of many colors and shapes and a variety of flowering times. Natural flower-rich habitats may have fifty or a hundred species, but for most foraging areas fifteen to twenty carefully chosen plant species will provide a good foundation from which a richer habitat can develop as the plants grow and spread or are supplemented with subsequent plantings. According to Gordon Frankie of the University of California, when eight or more species of appropriate plants

A site with a diversity of native plants that provide flowers throughout the season supports a wide range of pollinators. Edward S. Ross.

are grouped together, they tend to attract a significantly greater abundance and diversity of bee species. His researchers also found that native plants are four times more likely to attract native bees than are non-native plants. Finally, it is best to plant the flowers in patches of at least three to four feet in diameter.

Wherever you are planting, your foraging habitat should have four important characteristics:

♦ **It should incorporate a succession of flowers in order to provide blooms throughout the entire growing season.**

♦ **It should have several different species in bloom at any one time.**

♦ **It should combine annuals and perennials.**

♦ **It should be free of pesticides.**

A more diverse forage area attracts more pollinators because different insect species prefer different flowers. The size of the pollinators themselves, the size and shape of their mouthparts, and the accessibility of nectar or pollen within the flower are all factors in determining their preferences. Many species of bees can feed from open flowers such as asters and fennel that have a simple structure and easily accessible nectar, but some bees, which have long tongues or are big enough to push petals aside, seem to prefer more complex flowers such as lupine and salvia in which the nectar is hidden deep inside.

Another reason for providing a diversity of flowers is that the pollen preference of bees varies. Polylectic bees will gather pollen from many plants, but oligolectic bees collect their pollen from just a few kinds of flowers and monolectic bees from only one.

Flies, like bees, display a diversity of tongue lengths and associated flower preferences, although most have short mouthparts for which open flowers are best suited. Butterflies and moths, with their long tongues, can reach nectar in either simple or complex flowers. Beetles often feed at blooms where the nectar is accessible and there is plenty of landing space, and to which they are attracted by a pungent scent, such as that of western spicebush.

Some flowers have complex shapes, with the nectar and pollen accessible only to pollinators of the right size or with long enough tongues. Lupines (*Lupinus* sp.), for example, have a flower structure suitable for bumble bees. Jeff Owens / Metalmark Images.

In addition to selecting a range of flower shapes, colors, and flowering times, it is important to remember that, because native plants evolved along with native insects, they are the best food sources. In what has been described as a "mutualistic dance," flowers evolved to achieve the most effective pollen transfer and pollinator insects evolved to forage more efficiently. If there are already many native plant species at the site, you may not need to add more; simply watch for weeds and pull them. In most situations, however, you will probably need to augment with additional plants or seed.

THE IMPORTANCE OF COLOR

It is the color of a flower that attracts the attention of most passing pollinators. Petals are, in essence, signs advertising the availability of food (and provide a platform on which the insect can land in order to feed). It is believed that most bees and other pollinators locate potential floral hosts from a distance by the saturated colors of blossoms against the green foliage background, and are aided by scents as they get closer. Not surprisingly, pollinators see a considerable spectrum of colors and have both innate and learned color preferences. Flies will visit a wide range of colors, but seem most attracted to white and yellow. Bees also visit many colors, but are strongly attracted to blues and purples and are blind to red. Beetles, butterflies, and diurnal moths will visit many colors, including red. Some pollinators, such as nocturnal moths, may locate flowers from greater distances by their sweet fragrances, although night-blooming plants usually have white, cream, or pale green flowers, light colors that are visible at night.

Color, in the form of nectar guides—patterns of radiating lines or concentric circles on the petals—directs the insect to the nectar after it has landed. The color spectrum that bees see overlaps but does not match ours; they do not see red, but at the other end of the spectrum they can see ultraviolet, which is beyond human vision. The nectar guides on some flowers, including black-eyed Susans and buttercups, are ultraviolet, so insects see them and we do not.

Open flowers, such as this brittle bush (*Encelia farinosa*), have their nectar and pollen accessible to many pollinators. Stephen L. Buchmann.

Non-Floral Nutrition

Nectar and pollen are not the only foods sought out by pollinators. Some species of adult butterflies, for example, also get sugars from overripe fruit, so if you have fruit trees, let some fruit rot on the ground. Alternatively, you can place cut pieces of fruit—oranges, bananas, and peaches are especially appealing—in the garden for butterflies to find.

Muddy puddles, animal carcasses, and dung also provide vital nutrients that nectar alone cannot. You may not want to scavenge for fresh road kill for your garden (although dead animals have value in wild areas), but a damp patch of sand is easy to provide, even in a small space. Fill a shallow depression with sand; then dampen it and allow it to dry out each day. Or, if you have a drip irrigation system, allow one of the nozzles to create a damp place for butterflies. For low-tech solutions, make a pinhole in the bottom of a one-gallon plastic milk jug and set it out to form a moist area in the garden, or simply allow an outdoor faucet to drip (though in areas of low rainfall or drought a dripping faucet may not be appropriate).

Echo spring azures (*Celastrina ladon echo*), like many butterflies (particularly males), regularly drink at muddy puddles and animal scat, even carcasses, to get essential nutrients. Edward S. Ross.

Older, heirloom varieties can be combined with other native plants in a garden flower bed to provide foraging throughout the season. *Sedum spectabile*, often called ice plant or showy stonecrop, is a good late-summer nectar source. Matthew Shepherd.

NATIVE FLOWERS AND OLD-TIME FAVORITES

Native plants are usually the best choice to attract native pollinators not only because they evolved together, but also because the plants are well adapted to your local growing conditions, soils, and climate, and can thrive with minimum attention. While we recommend using native plants, heirloom varieties of non-native perennials and herbs can be planted as well to create attractive flower borders and beds in back yards, office campuses, and city parks. This is preferable to planting modern horticultural flower varieties and double-flowered hybrids, which, though they may be suited to local conditions, are likely to produce less nectar or pollen as an unintended consequence of having been bred to produce showy blooms. In fact, some of these magnificent blooms produce no pollen or nectar at all, and may even have non-functional sexual parts.

See Appendix D for a more complete list of native plants that attract pollinators. You can also find some plant lists for specific regions on the Xerces Society's web site, www.xerces.org. Or contact your local chapter of the Native Plant Society, Master Gardener volunteers working with the your county extension service, or native plant nurseries. Some city bureaus have lists of local native plants or botanists who can advise you. The web site of the Lady Bird Johnson Wildflower Research Center gives state-by-state listings of wildflower organizations and other resources. The National Gardening Association may also be able to advise you.

Invasive Non-Native Species

There are many compelling reasons to go native; not least is that some non-native species can be terribly destructive, and we do not always know in advance which ones they will be. Invasive non-native species are the scourge of our nation's parks, forests, fields, and farms. They are a leading cause of the loss of biodiversity; only development and agriculture are more destructive. And non-native weeds cost our nation billions of dollars each year both in the direct costs of weed control and in the value of lost crop production. Not all non-native species are invasive, but with so many native species to choose from, as well as non-native species that are known to not be invasive, there is no reason to plant something that may run rampant.

Some non-native species that have become invasive were originally planted with the idea of stabilizing soil or providing color along the highway; others were planted by settlers nostalgic for home. But the effect has been that plants such as purple loosestrife (*Lythrum salicaria*) and Scotch broom (*Cytisus scoparius*) have overwhelmed other vegetation, reduced biological diversity, and destroyed pollinator habitat. Even some plants that are widely promoted as being beneficial for insects should be used with care. The purple-flowered butterfly bush (*Buddleja davidii*), for example, is widely sold by nurseries and touted as a butterfly magnet; however, planted in congenial conditions, such as warm riparian areas, it can spread quickly and become a menace.

Invasive species, particularly non-native ones, often look beautiful, but they can harm wildlife habitat by out-competing the native plants and reducing diversity. Scotch broom (*Cytisus scoparius*) was brought here from Europe and is now a significant problem throughout the Northwest. Mace Vaughan.

PLANTS OR SEEDS?

You've decided what to plant to create your habitat. The next question—whether you are transforming a lawn into a flower-rich prairie, planting a flower border in a garden, or adding foraging plants to an existing natural area—is whether to use container-grown plants or start from seed. Established plants have the advantage that they will more likely survive drought and competition from weeds in the first year, and thus will reward you and local pollinator populations with forage habitat sooner than seeds will. Perennials in particular may take a couple of years to reach their peak blooming; annuals, by their very nature, flower the first year. Container-grown annuals are preferable when used in an area with established vegetation, where tiny seedlings may be crowded out by grasses and other existing plants. If you have a greenhouse or space on a warm windowsill, you can sow seeds in trays and grow your own planting stock.

Seeds cost much less than plants and may make economic sense if you are working on a large scale—landscaping a new park, golf course, or business campus, for instance. And some species, such as poppies, do not transplant well but are easy to grow from seed, which is preferable regardless of the scale. Also, for some plants, such as a native species that is not in high demand, seed will be the only source available. In that case, check with a local nursery that specializes in native plants; it may be able to get the seed and start it for you. Finally, some seeds germinate easily and will grow in most situations without difficulty, though for other plants the failure rate with seed is so high that any cost savings is offset by the additional maintenance and replacement work necessary. Again, the best way to be sure is to check with your nursery.

If you are using seed to cheaply and swiftly develop large areas of species-rich, prairie-like habitat on bare ground, you'll need to think

Red flowers, particularly tubular ones like this beardtongue (*Penstemon* sp.), attract hummingbirds; many butterflies and some bees will drink nectar from them as well. Stephen L. Buchmann.

about the best way of sowing it, which will depend on the site's location, topography, and size. Broadcasting seed by hand may be the best, simplest method for small areas. Before you broadcast, mix the seeds with sand to get an even spread and to help keep birds from eating the seeds. For larger areas, planting with a seed drill or hydro-seeding (especially on steep or otherwise inaccessible sites) might be the best options; for these applications it may be necessary to hire a contractor. After seeding, rake or harrow the area to cover the seeds. You may then want to add a layer of straw mulch or other suitable material to stabilize the soil and reduce erosion. If the site is near a body of water, erosion fences may be required by local environmental codes, and should be installed anyway to protect the water from siltation.

How Many Plants Should You Plant?

The next step is to work out how many plants or how much seed you'll need. For a yard or garden, simply consider the size of the mature plants and their needs for sunlight, shade, and moisture, and plant accordingly. In a natural area, where you may have the space to create a plant community that can generate sufficient seed to replace plants that die, you may want to consult with your local nursery on how many plants you'll need in order to get a good start. Other factors to consider include your local conditions, the type of plants you're buying, and the time and energy you have for maintaining them.

Planting Patterns

To form the larger clusters that attract many pollinators, plant flowers to form blocks of colored blooms rather than scattered spots of color. It is best to plant several individuals of the same species together. If you wonder whether it works just as well to plant four different species of the same color—a red azalea, a red rose, a red poppy, and a red geranium, say—it does not; it is preferable to create a block of color with a single species. It is even better to group a single species of native plants, since the blooms of a particular native species will tend to vary little in color. Hybrids, on the other hand, are bred for their colors and often display a vast range. A single pack of lupine seed, for example, may yield blooms of many colors, while native lupines of the same species will all be the same color.

In school grounds, city parks, and golf courses—or in any area where you are replacing mown grass with pollinator habitat or enhancing existing wild areas by adding plants for forage—you will probably want to use container-grown plants. If you would like the area to look natural, distribute the plants randomly rather than in regularly spaced straight lines. To get the blocks of color you need to best attract pollinators, plant individual species in clumps of at least three to five.

When to Plant

Plants need time to get established, so knowing when to plant is important. In theory, container-grown plants can be planted when the ground is warm enough to dig. But planting times vary according to climatic conditions, so consult your local nursery or a garden book particular to your area. Whether you live in an area with a short growing season, in a rainy climate, or where drought prevails, you will want to time your planting to take advantage of rainfall. You will also want to use native plants that are adapted to the local conditions in order to reduce the need for irrigation, minimize maintenance, avoid costly replacement, and get the best results from your efforts.

Watering and Weeding

When your plants are in the ground, regular basic care—irrigation and weed control—is the key to their health. The general rule for irrigation is to water deeply once a week until the roots are well established. How long that takes will vary depending on the plants and your local growing conditions. (For irrigation information specific to

Sphinx moths (genus *Hyles*) hover in front of flowers while nectaring.
David Inouye.

your area and plants, read the label or seed package, or consult your
local nursery or general planting book.) Deep watering encourages
plants to develop deep roots that follow the water, resulting in plants
that are stronger and more able to withstand drought and competition from weeds. Drip hoses and soaker hoses are recommended because they provide moisture at the root level, conserving water that
would otherwise evaporate; drip hoses can be precisely directed to the
plants you are nurturing.

The growing conditions that are good for pollinator plants are
also good for weeds. The term "weed" refers to a plant that competes
for light, nutrients, and water with the plants that you want. It's a relative concept; a plant that is a weed in one place may not be a weed
in another. In the context of pollinator conservation, the issue be-
comes even more complicated because many plants that we commonly consider weeds, such as purple loosestrife and dandelions, are
excellent nectar sources for pollinators. That's why it is important to

keep in mind the big picture—the importance of protecting the over-all health of the ecosystem. From that perspective, purple loosestrife is a destructive weed. Indeed, a weed would be any invasive non-native species, even if it is a good plant for pollinators, because it de-grades the overall plant community by reducing the diversity of spe-cies. Many native plants provide fine nectar and coexist well with a diversity of plant species, and these should be encouraged.

To control weeds, especially in relatively small areas, there are ex-cellent alternatives to herbicides. Herbicides will damage your new plants as well as the weeds. A better way to address weeds, many of which are shallowly rooted annuals, is to irrigate no more than once a week; the soil surface dries out between waterings and weeds are less able to survive. Mulching in the first year after planting will also help control weeds, but it won't eliminate them completely. The most ef-fective way to get rid of perennial weeds is to pull or dig them out, getting as much of the roots as you can and, in order to cut off next year's supply, do it before the weeds go to flower and then to seed. An-

We tend to think first of bees and butterflies when we think of polli-nators, but a large variety of other insects, such as this long-horned bee-tle (*Typocerus zebra*), also have a significant role to play. It is important to take them into consideration in managing habitat. Arthur V. Evans.

nual weeds can be pulled or cut before they go to seed. Getting rid of weeds takes time, but if you are diligent and persistent, there will be many fewer each year.

Habitat Management

You may not be used to thinking of your yard or garden this way, but any patch of flowers that provides food for pollinator insects is a form of wildlife habitat. Fortunately, caring for a garden of pollinator-friendly plants is similar to tending a regular garden, though there are a few things you will want to do differently. With perennials, for example, removing the dead flowers will encourage more blooming—and thus more opportunity for your pollinators to forage. On the other hand, leaving dead stems rather than cutting them back at the end of the season will provide overwintering opportunities for pollinator insects. The dead growth can be removed the following spring as the plants again begin to grow.

Large-scale pollinator habitat connected with parks, school yards, golf courses, and wild areas will also require management, but the details will depend on the conditions you expect to maintain. In grassland plant communities, you may need to do periodic cutting or use controlled burns to keep scrub or forest from encroaching. Cutting or pulling woody plants to check their spread may be the best strategy for most areas; burning as a management practice should be approached with care and expert advice.

A wide range of insects—including butterflies, beetles, and bees—lay eggs on or overwinter inside plant stems, so avoid cutting or burning an entire site at one time. To ensure that all areas are cut and that there are always areas of viable overwintering habitat each year, divide the site into patches that can be managed over a rotation period of four or more years. Longer rotation is preferable, but it may not always be practical to divide a small site into multiple management units. More information about managing habitat on a large scale can be found in the last section of Chapter 6, beginning on page 72.

8

Nesting and Egg-Laying Sites

Pollinator populations benefit most from flower-rich, pesticide-free foraging areas if there are also suitable egg-laying or nesting sites close by. In fact, a lack of nesting sites may be a more significant limitation on healthy pollinator populations than a lack of flowers. Addressing this need will not entail much extra work, for in providing good foraging habitat you are already supplying suitable egg-laying sites for many pollinators.

Most insects are particular about where they lay their eggs, and will seek a spot that will provide food and shelter for the young after the eggs hatch. Flies and beetles lay eggs in many different sorts of niches, and habitat that is good for foraging adults also supports many of the needs of the larvae. A number of flies and beetles, for example, are predators or parasites as larvae—some beetle larvae hunt through leaf litter for their prey; some flower fly larvae feed on aphids; and the larvae of small-headed flies are internal parasites of spiders. You probably already support healthy populations of the organisms these pollinator larvae feed on, so there is little more you need to do for them.

However, other pollinators—including butterflies, certain species of flies and beetles, and bees—require particular plants or conditions for nesting. Butterflies lay eggs only on or near specific host plants, ones that their caterpillars will eat. Some flies and beetles require rotting logs in which to lay eggs. Bees and some wasps are the only pollinator insects that build nests—either in holes in trees or shrubs, or in burrows or cavities in the ground—and then provision them with nectar and pollen for their brood. The locations of these nests must be suitable, which generally means that they should be sunny but sheltered from wind and rain.

Protecting Natural Nesting Sites for Bees

Nearly 70 percent of the solitary bee species—as well as all of the social sweat bees—nest in the ground; their nests can be shallow or deep, a single passageway or multiple branching tunnels. Of the remaining 30 percent, most nest in beetle holes in dead trees or limbs. A few, such as the carpenter bees, use their powerful mandibles to chew tunnels into stems or wood that are relatively soft, such as century plant, yucca, blackberry, redwood, or pine. Some bee species even construct small pot-like cells from pebbles and resin on the side of a stone or plant stem, or occupy empty snail shells. Bumble bees need a cavity in which to nest, typically under a grass tussock or in an abandoned rodent burrow.

About two-thirds of the bee species of North America nest in tunnels in the ground. Suitable sites vary from small exposures of bare earth on a bank to flat expanses of salty soil. Matthew Shepherd.

If you insist on keeping things too tidy, you may lose bee nesting habitat. Bark mulch used to cover bare ground can prevent bees from burrowing, especially if there is landscape fabric under it. Cutting all of the patches of rough grass can deprive bumble bees of a home, and removing logs, dead limbs, or snags (standing dead trees) reduces the number of natural nesting sites. Often snags are removed in the name of public safety, even if they pose no risk. An arborist can advise on whether a snag is really a hazard; if you can leave it, it will provide excellent nesting habitat for bees, wasps, beetles, flies, birds, and bats.

CREATING ARTIFICIAL NESTING SITES

If you cannot preserve intact nesting habitats for bees, you can create —perhaps even inadvertently—artificial nests that supply the conditions they need. In spring, for instance, you may find mason bees nesting in the ends of an unused hose or pipe, in bamboo canes stored for the winter, or between the wooden shingles on your house. If the location and design are right, bees may move in.

You can also be more deliberate. Recently, many people have become interested in the blue orchard bee (*Osmia lignaria*)—also called the orchard mason bee—as a garden and orchard pollinator, and have constructed or purchased bee nesting blocks (pieces of lumber with holes of a uniform size drilled in them). Many thousands of bee nesting blocks are sold each year in the United States, along with about 300,000 blue orchard bees. These are fine, but it is very important not to import bees that are not local, especially into a wild area, even if they are represented as being the same species as local bees. It is far better to place an empty block appropriately as described below, and let the locally resident bees find it. This will help strengthen the native bee populations.

If you want to save some expense and give yourself the pleasure of making your own bee nesting habitat, you can create one that attracts a variety of bee species by making a block—or one of the other structures that we describe below—with holes of various sizes. Instant

There are many places where you can buy nesting blocks for blue orchard bees. These have a single hole size of the diameter preferred by these early-spring bees, though the blocks will also be used by some leafcutter bees. Matthew Shepherd.

diversity! That said, it is better to buy a nesting block than not to have bee nesting habitat at all. Indeed, bee "condos" are sprouting in gardens and back yards almost as fast as the plants the bees are intended to pollinate; clearly, many people understand the value and pleasure of attracting native bees to their yards and gardens.

Nests for Wood-Nesting Bees

To fulfill the general nesting requirements of wood-nesting bees, your nest should meet these criteria:

◆ **It should provide a range of hole sizes, in order to attract a variety of bee species.** The females of different species of bees prefer different diameters and depths of hole, and a nesting structure that offers an assortment of hole sizes will attract a greater diversity of bees.

- **It should face the morning sun.** Direct sunshine in the morning will help bees warm themselves up to flight temperature, so place wooden nests for solitary bees facing southeast or east, allowing the morning sun to fall on the entrance holes. The bees also prefer shelter from direct rain and—particularly in hot climates—from the midday sun, as might be found under the eaves of a house or garden shed.

- **It should be fixed to a firm support.** Affix your bee nest to a firm and stable support as bees will detect the vibrations caused by a wobbly post, and nest elsewhere. The actual height from the ground does not much matter, although if the nest is too low, rain splash may dampen it. Anywhere from 2 to 6 feet (0.6 to 1.8 meters) from the ground is good. We like 4 feet (1.25 meters)—perfect for close-up bee watching from the comfort of a lawn chair.

Wooden Blocks

The standard commercially made bee nest is a wooden block with a lot of holes in it, which you can buy in many garden centers and wild-bird shops. The holes are usually 5/16 inch (8 millimeters) in diameter, the size preferred by blue orchard bees, a species that is active only in the spring and will not pollinate your later-flowering fruits and vegetables. It's very simple to make a block yourself, and one that will accommodate the needs of many different species that are active throughout the summer months.

We recommend using preservative-free dimensional lumber: a 4 by 4—which is actually 3½ inches (9 centimeters) square—for blocks with smaller diameter holes, or a 4 by 6—actually 3½ by 5½ inches (9 by 14 centimeters)—for blocks with larger diameter holes. You can also use a rough block of wood instead, as long as it is about these dimensions or bigger in cross-section. The length of the block is less important, but 8 inches (20 centimeters) or more is good.

In one side, drill a series of nest holes of appropriate sizes and depths. Nesting holes should be between 3/32 and 3/8 inch (2.5 and

10 millimeters) in diameter. Holes of ¼ inch (6.5 millimeters) or less in diameter should be 3 to 5 inches (8 to 13 centimeters) deep. Holes larger than ¼ inch should be 5 to 6 inches (13 to 15 centimeters) deep. The female bee controls the gender of her offspring, and always finishes the nest with a few male brood cells. A deeper hole ensures space for more female brood cells.

The holes should be about ¾ inch (19 millimeters) from center to center, and no closer than that to the edges. Attach a backing board if you drill all the way through your block, because bees will not use a hole that is open at both ends. With smaller diameter drill bits, you may not be able to achieve the 3-inch (8-centimeter) minimum recommended depth. If that is the case, simply drill as deeply as you can; bees that use holes of smaller diameters will often nest successfully in ones that aren't as deep.

Bees may avoid a rough interior, so your holes should be perpendicular to the wood's grain, and drilled with a sharp bit. You can buy

By making your own block with several different hole sizes you can offer nesting sites to a diversity of bee species. Mace Vaughan.

paper straws to line the holes, although it may be hard to find straws that fit all diameters. Paint the outer tips of the straws black or red to help attract bees. (The web site of the U.S. Department of Agriculture Bee Biology and Systematics Laboratory has an extensive list of straw suppliers; see Appendix C.)

The exterior of the block can be rustic or fancy, and any color you like. The bees won't mind as long as the holes are of appropriate diameters and depths, snug enough for nesting females. You can attach an overhanging roof to provide additional shelter.

An alternative to a wooden block is to drill holes in a log, then erect it like a fence post to simulate a beetle-tunneled snag. You can also simply drill holes in a stump.

Stem Bundles

If you don't have a drill, or if you are doing a project with young children, one option is to make nests from bundles of hollow stems. Bamboo, teasel, and common reed are good choices because their hollow stems are naturally blocked at the stem nodes (usually indicated by a ridge). Cut each stem below the nodes to create a handful of tubes

Tying hollow stems into a bundle is an easy way to make nests for wood-nesting bees. This one is made from teasel stems, but bamboo, common reed, and sumac can also be used. Matthew Shepherd.

each with one open end. Strap the tubes together into a tight bundle with wire, string, or tape, making certain that the closed ends of the stems are all at the same end of the bundle. A variation on this is to tightly pack the stems—open ends out—into a tin can, paper milk carton, or short section of PVC pipe. The bundles should be placed in a sheltered location with the stems horizontal to the ground and the holes facing east to get the morning sun.

You can also use freshly cut twigs and stems of pithy and soft-centered plants, such as box elder, elderberry, sumac, raspberry, agave, or yucca. Carpenter bees both large and small will chew the pith to create their nesting tunnels.

Nesting Stakes

Another alternative is to create nesting stakes. Again using a pithy stemmed plant, cut straight stems 24 to 30 inches (60 to 75 centimeters) in length. These should be between $\frac{1}{2}$ and 1 inch (12.5 and 25 millimeters) in diameter. About 12 inches (30 centimeters) from one end, drill a small hole $\frac{3}{16}$ inch (5 millimeters) or less in diameter about half-way through the stake, so that the hole reaches into the central pith. Sharpen the other end of the stake and push it about 6 inches (15 centimeters) into the ground.

Nesting Materials

Besides the nesting holes themselves, different bee species need different materials to construct their brood cells and seal the nests. A few wood-nesting bees secrete a cellophane-like substance to divide brood cells, but most use materials they gather, such as pieces of leaf or petal, mud, fine pebbles, or tree resins. The chances are that these are already present in your area, but if you provide a diversity of native plants and some mud puddles, you can guarantee it.

Maintenance of Nests for Wood-Nesting Bees

Whether your nesting sites are wooden blocks, twig bundles, or other materials, a major maintenance issue is whether or when to clean out the holes. In general, cleaning will help to reduce parasites, fungi, and diseases that might affect the developing bees in their brood cells.

The big advantage of using paper straws to line nesting holes is that the nest block will be easy to clean. At the end of summer, use tweezers, forceps, or hemostats to pull out the straws containing brood cells and dormant pupae, and carefully store them in a cool place over the winter, perhaps in an unheated but frost-free shed or garage, or even in your refrigerator. The straws should be in a ventilated container to prevent mold. Be very gentle with the occupied straws. The empty blocks can then be washed with a mild bleach solution, dried, and stored for the winter.

In the spring, do not put the occupied straws back into the blocks; instead, insert new straws to create clean nesting sites and return the blocks to their previous locations. Meanwhile, take the occupied straws from storage, bundle them and place them in a protected, east-facing location close to the clean blocks. After the bees emerge, dispose of the abandoned straws so they are not reused.

Cleaning stem bundles and nesting stakes—or a wooden block with holes that have not been lined with straws—is difficult because there may be no time in the year when many of the holes are unoccupied and thus safe to clean. It is better to make new nests each year to put alongside your existing ones. To limit the build-up of damaging pests, destroy or re-drill the oldest nesting blocks every three or four years. You want to first let the bees emerge from these nests, so in the spring place the blocks in a box that has a single exit hole, ½ inch in diameter. When the bees emerge they will leave the box through the exit hole and will not return to the nests. To ensure that they will disperse to a new block, place the box on the north side of a shed or fence, or on the shady side of a hedge or tree. When the plugs sealing the nests have been broken, the bees will have emerged. You can either remove and destroy the blocks, or clean them with a mild bleach solution and redrill the holes. More elaborate ways to rid nest blocks of parasites are described in guides on rearing blue orchard bees. (See Appendix C).

NESTING SITES FOR GROUND-NESTING BEES

While it's fun to fashion bee blocks for wood-nesting bees, most of our native bees nest in the ground in areas that are sunny, well drained, and either bare or partly vegetated. There are many ground-nesting bee species, and different conditions—from flat ground to vertical banks, packed earth to loose soil—will attract different species.

Because ground-nesting bees prefer bare ground, the first thing to do is clear the vegetation from a space as small as a foot or two square, but preferably several yards across. It can be level or sloping, but it should be well drained and in an open, sunny place. A sunny bank is ideal. Place a few rocks in the cleared area; they will retain heat and the bees will bask on them.

Many bees prefer to nest in sand or a mixture of sand and loam that is soft enough to dig in and stable enough that it won't collapse, and that drains easily so the nest won't flood. Simply dig a pit two or three feet deep and as large as you have space for, and fill it with pale, fine-grained sand or a mixture of sand and loam. If the ground is damp or is too hard to dig, make a pile of sand (or sand and loam mixture) to create better nesting conditions. If you have enough space, pile a few hundred pounds of sand to create various depths and slopes for nesting. For a neater look in more formal landscapes, make raised beds edged with lumber or bricks and filled with sand and loam. A simple approach is to fill a planter box, which has the advantage of being self contained and therefore mobile, and place it in a sunny spot. It can be tilted to any angle—if the contents are sufficiently compacted—to provide nesting surfaces from horizontal to vertical. With a selection of planters at different angles you may attract a range of bees.

Adobe Walls

In desert or semi-arid areas, the ground-nesting equivalent of a wooden nest block is a wall made from adobe bricks. Construct the wall with the front facing east or southeast to catch the morning sun, and drill nesting holes between $3/32$ and $1/2$ inch (2.5 and 13 millimeters) in diameter and 3 to 6 inches (8 to 15 centimeters) deep into the face. Holes that are $1/4$ inch (6.5 millimeters) or more in diameter should be at least 5 inches (13 centimeters) deep. If you build the wall with a wooden backing and put a roof or plank over the top layer of bricks, it will last longer. Adobe may not hold up well in a wet climate, but you can buy adobe bricks that have a stabilizing plasticizer mixed in. As with wooden blocks, adobe walls can be as decorative or rustic as you like.

Maintenance of Nests for Ground-Nesting Bees

In general, it is important that ground-nesting sites get good sun. This might mean that you will need to trim back bushes or trees from time to time, and keep weeds and moss from becoming too dense. Try not to walk across the site while adult bees are active and, during the rest of the year, remember that buried under the ground are possibly hundreds of bees. For this reason, it is best not to dig deeply into the soil unless you have to.

NESTING BOXES FOR BUMBLE BEES

Unlike solitary bees, which can be very particular about hole diameters, bumble bees are flexible in their nesting needs. All they are looking for is a dry, warm cavity of a suitable size that contains soft nesting materials and an entrance hole less than an inch (25 millimeters) in diameter. Anything that fits those criteria can become a bumble bee nest.

A simple wooden box, with internal dimensions of about 7 by 7 by 7 inches (18 by 18 by 18 centimeters) and made from preservative-free lumber, will work. Drill a few ventilation holes near the top—covered with window screen to deter ants—and some drainage holes in the bottom. Make an entrance tunnel from $3/4$-inch (19-millimeter) diameter plastic pipe, marked on the outside with a contrasting color, and fill the box with soft bedding material, such as upholsterer's cotton or short lengths of soft unraveled string. The box must be weathertight; if the nest gets damp, the larvae may become too cold, and mold and fungus will grow.

Some designs for bumble bee nest boxes are for double-chambered homes. Such luxury is not necessary; any suitably located box or container of an appropriate size, with an entrance, drainage and ventilation holes, and nesting materials, may be used. Even a small six-pack Styrofoam cooler outfitted with a short length of garden hose for the entrance will work. Some of the earliest experiments in creating artificial nests used metal watering cans buried underground with the spouts serving as entrance tunnels.

Unlike other bee species, bumble bees don't require morning sun. They can warm themselves by vibrating their wing muscles on cold mornings; in fact, they can raise their internal temperatures to nearly

Watching the foraging behaviors of bumble bees on flowers is entertaining and safe. When they are at their nests, however, some species can be feisty in defense of the colony. Nests are usually located in underground cavities or in a grass tussock, but bees will readily move into an artificial nesting box. Edward S. Ross.

110 degrees Fahrenheit (45 degrees Centigrade). Simply place the nest in a dry, undisturbed area that has some obvious landmarks (a fence post, rock, or building) to aid bee navigation; these are important to bees returning from foraging. Nesting boxes that are at ground level or slightly buried are the most attractive to queens of many species. Boxes placed on the surface should be level and stable. If you are burying your box, add an entrance pipe extension that gently slopes up to the surface, and where it surfaces clear the vegetation from an area a few inches across.

Most bumble bees are very gentle creatures, especially when visiting flowers. A few species can be aggressive in defending their nests, in particular *Bombus pennsylvanicus* in the East and *Bombus pennsylvanicus sonorus* in the Southwest, both fairly common species. It is not unusual for bumble bees to find nesting sites under a deck or shed and never cause problems, but it is a good idea to locate nests away from places where people will be active, avoid unnecessary disturbance, and be cautious when close to a nest. This does not mean you should not put nests in your garden or never go near them, but don't put them within two or three yards of paths, play areas, patios, or similar places.

Most bumble bees will not be threatened by your presence and will even allow you to lift the lid occasionally and look inside the nest box. If you intend to do this, however, it is best to make a plexiglas inner lid for the nest, so you can lift the roof without unnecessarily disturbing the occupants. Be careful when you approach the nest or try to look inside; avoid jarring it or breathing on the entrance. Even gentle species might interpret such actions as harassment and respond accordingly.

The best time to install a bumble bee nest box is in early spring, when the first queens have emerged from hibernation and are searching for a nest site; in many areas, this is when the willows first start blooming. Once the nest is in place, be patient. It may take weeks for a bee to move in, if one ever does. On average, bumble bees will occupy perhaps one box in three.

Maintenance of Bumble Bee Nests

Bumble bee nests require little maintenance. Watch your boxes through the spring and early summer. Any above-ground boxes that are unoccupied by late July can be removed, cleaned, and put into storage until the following spring; this is not vital, and if you have a lot of boxes on a large site it may not be practical. In late fall or early winter inspect all the boxes that have been occupied. Remove the old nests, clean them, and make any repairs. Cleaning the boxes with a mild bleach solution will help to reduce parasites and diseases in the nests. The following spring, add fresh nesting material to all the boxes.

LARVAL HOST PLANTS FOR BUTTERFLIES

The idea of growing a plant so that a caterpillar can eat it might seem odd. But in the big picture of creating healthy habitat, it makes perfect sense. Some butterfly and moth caterpillars are highly specialized in their food needs. It is important to provide their larval host plants, given that it is at the caterpillar stage that these insects grow most rapidly. A monarch caterpillar, for example, may be only a sixteenth of an inch long when newly hatched; within two or three weeks it can grow thirty-fold, to two inches in length. The range of plants on which the females of different butterfly species will lay their eggs varies enormously. The monarch has a very restricted range of larval hosts, laying her eggs only on the milkweed plant; the anise swallowtail, at the other extreme, is known to use over sixty different plants from the carrot family as larval hosts.

To provide the appropriate host plants, you first have to know what butterflies you would be likely to find in your local area, and then match their larval requirements with local plant species. For example, planting milkweed in areas of the Pacific Northwest west of the Cascade Range is highly unlikely to attract monarch butterflies, because they are rare in that region. On the other hand, anise swallowtails are common along the West Coast, so planting fennel or dill would be likely to attract them. Appendix D lists larval host plants for common butterflies. It is not a definitive list, and we recommend that you contact your local nursery, native plant society, or county extension service, or study a regional butterfly guide book, such as *Butterflies of Cascadia*, by Robert Michael Pyle, for information particular to your local area. Other good sources include *Butterfly Gardening: Creating Summer Magic in Your Garden*, by the Xerces Society and the Smithsonian Institution, and *Butterfly Gardening: Creating a Butterfly Haven in Your Garden*, by Thomas Emmel.

FLIES AND BEETLES

There is a huge diversity of pollinating flies and beetles, but their egg-laying and larval needs are likely to be provided for if you focus on managing habitat—food, nesting, and egg-laying sites—for bees and butterflies. The foraging plants you provide for butterflies and bees will be home to spiders and aphids, the preferred larval food, respectively, of small-headed flies and many syrphid flies. The larvae of some syrphid flies live in the bottom of bumble bee nests, and the larvae of bee flies are parasites of ground-nesting solitary bees, so providing for these bees takes care of other pollinators in the process. Introduce some dead wood and leave a few untidy corners, and you will have seen to most of the egg-laying needs of the pollinator flies and the nutritional needs of their larvae.

Most of the habitat requirements for pollinating beetles will also be met in the process of managing for bees and butterflies. The larvae of soldier beetles and soft-winged flower beetles hunt for prey in soil, leaf litter, moss, and similar places. The larvae of metallic wood-boring beetles and long-horned beetles usually live in the wood of weakened trees. If you have the little extra space it takes, as well as trees that are generally healthy, think twice before removing snags and dying trees that provide benefits both for these pollinator beetles and for populations of wood-nesting bees whose females construct their nests within the beetle tunnels.

Butterfly larvae are particular about which plants they can eat, so pollinator habitat needs the right host plants. The caterpillar of the American lady (*Vanessa virginiensis*) prefers pussytoes (*Antennaria*) and pearly everlasting (*Anaphalis*), shown here. Edward S. Ross.

When you've addressed the dietary, nesting, and egg-laying needs of pollinators, you might be ready to rest and to enjoy what you've created by noticing what you have attracted. When the weather permits and the flowers are blooming, treat yourself to a relaxing hour or two observing the antics of a bee struggling into a flower, then emerging with its body dappled with pollen, which it will leave at its subsequent stops; or watch as a butterfly pokes its proboscis into a lupine. Can you identify the nesting materials bees are bringing to the stem bundles? As you observe, questions may occur to you, such as where do these creatures go to pupate, and what happens when there are no flowers or the weather turns cold?

9
Pupation and Overwintering Sites

Pollinators, like most insects, require different things of their habitat depending upon their life stage and the time of year. In addition to when they are active—as larvae and adults—there are three periods when they are inactive. Two are life stages, the egg and the pupa; the third is the season when conditions are inhospitable to activity and the insect undergoes diapause, or hibernation. Often, two inactive periods coincide and the insect passes through an inhospitable season as egg or pupa. In many areas, diapause occurs on a regular and predicable annual basis that corresponds to changes in temperature, rainfall or the lack thereof, and the availability of flowers and other food sources. For each of the three periods of inactivity, an insect requires a sheltered place.

BEES

For most bees, pupation and overwintering needs are both served by the nest. Solitary bees spend most of the year in their brood cells, passing through the stages of egg, larva, and pupa. They emerge in the spring or summer and spend only a few weeks active as adults. Some species of solitary bees, such as small carpenter bees, emerge at the end of the summer and overwinter as adults, usually in their original nests. In contrast, most bumble bees and sweat bees die at the end of summer, leaving only the fertilized queens to hibernate. The queen bumble bee does not hibernate in her nest, which by then is likely to be moldy and maggot-infested; rather, she survives the winter by burrowing into soil or finding shelter in leaf litter or behind bark.

Butterflies and Moths

The needs of Lepidoptera are slightly more complex, as these insects may require separate places to pupate and to overwinter. Some species complete pupation in only a few weeks during the summer. Others overwinter as pupae, perhaps wrapped in cocoons or buried underground (in the case of many moths), or surrounded by a hardened chrysalis (as with butterflies). Pupation normally occurs in such places as on tall grass, bushes, trees, fence posts, or the outside of a house, or inside a pile of leaves or sticks. To find such a safe place, caterpillars may crawl many yards from their larval host plants. Keeping some untidy corners and piles of woody debris in your garden will give these creatures a place to go. Depending on the species, butterflies may survive the winter in any of the four life stages of egg, caterpillar, pupa, or adult. For those species that pass the winter as eggs or caterpillars, the best protection you can offer is to leave their larval host plants undisturbed during those months.

Many pollinator insects have life stages during which they are dormant, and need sheltered, undisturbed places. This is a chrysalis of an anise swallowtail (*Papilio zelicaon*) on a twig. Mace Vaughan.

Overwintering as Adults

Although only a handful of such long-lived butterflies as anglewings and tortoiseshells overwinter as adults, many stores sell overwintering boxes for butterflies. Some are ornate and make attractive additions to a garden, but there is no evidence that the boxes work, at least not for butterflies. Spiders will move in, so the boxes do have some benefit for your garden. But there are some more effective ways that you can help butterflies survive winter.

Under natural conditions, butterflies that overwinter as adults are likely to take shelter in tree cavities, under logs, behind loose bark, under rocks, or within evergreen foliage. Human activities have inadvertently created other viable sites, such as stone walls, buildings, and fences.

It is easy to purposefully create an overwintering site by building a pile of logs or rocks, or by planting evergreen climbers or trees. Logs should be stacked criss-crossed with gaps of at least 3 to 4 inches (8 to 10 centimeters). Covering the stack with a sheet of plastic or roofing felt will offer protection from rain and wind. If you prefer, you can disguise it by planting nectar and larval plants around it or a creeper over it.

Rock piles are harder to make, but may be less obtrusive. They need to be constructed and placed to give shelter from prevailing winds and rain. You don't have to use natural rock; this can be an opportunity to dispose of chunks of unwanted concrete. Evergreen climbers—preferably native, though in a yard or garden, non-native varieties that are non-invasive will also work—growing over walls or buildings can offer good overwintering niches, as can the dense foliage of conifer trees.

Overwintering sites, like all pollinator habitat, require some maintenance. You may have to re-attach the covering if it blows loose, replace logs that have rotted away, or prune back climbers. It's best to do these chores in the summer, so that you don't disturb the sites from late fall to early spring, when they are likely to be occupied.

Migration

Migrating species—in particular monarch butterflies, which over-winter in Mexico and California—require foraging resources in their summer breeding sites and secure locations in which to overwinter, as well as a corridor of nectar-rich habitat patches along their migration routes, across landscapes altered by agriculture and development. Because monarch butterflies are very specific in their overwintering requirements, they are now limited to a few remnants of forest in the mountains of central Mexico (where more than 95 percent of them overwinter) and isolated tree groves in California. These places must be protected if the monarchs are to survive.

To sustain them on their journeys, the monarchs require nectar for energy. On their return north in the spring, they also need native milkweed on which to lay their eggs. These needs can be met with stepping-stone habitat patches, which may be nothing more than the "weeds" growing in a field margin or on a road verge. A tolerant farmer or road maintenance crew that leaves these areas to grow rather than cutting or spraying them may help provide the feeding or egg-laying resources these migrating pollinators need. So too with each small area of pollinator habitat that you create; a patch of milkweed left untouched may reward you with the sight of a newly emerged monarch warming its wings on a spring morning so that it might fly.

10

Conclusion

Pollinating insects are small and easily overlooked, but what they contribute to the lives of human beings, wild animals, and plants is enormous. Fundamental grassroots action is needed to protect these populations. You can help by providing them with habitat in which to nest and forage. The ideas in the *Pollinator Conservation Handbook* can be adapted to fit any location, from a small urban back yard to an office campus, city park, or natural area.

As you think about both where to site your pollinator habitat and how much effort you are prepared to make, consider that there are a range of possibilities, and that taking any action, however modest,

Nesting blocks may be occupied quickly, with different species of bee using different materials to seal the finished nests. This nesting block was built and painted by River Black, age nine. Mace Vaughan.

Planting flowers rich in nectar and pollen serves both to add beauty to our landscapes and to support pollinator insects such as these small carpenter bees, genus *Ceratina*. Edward S. Ross.

is better than taking none at all. Habitat for pollinators has a few basic requirements: a flower-rich foraging area, a variety of bee nesting sites, and suitable plants and places for other insects to lay their eggs.

Sometimes, simple steps can be the most successful and the most immediately satisfying. Either wooden nesting blocks or bundles of hollow stems can attract bees within days of being installed. A patch of suitable flowering plants is a fast magnet for butterflies, bees, flies, and beetles. Increase the scope and size of your pollinator habitat, and you will add to the diversity, abundance, and productivity of your garden. If you use pesticides, consider the alternatives; if your neighbors use pesticides, work with them to find a better way.

If you are working on a large-scale project, or one that involves public land, plan ahead, take one step at a time, involve other people, and enjoy yourself. Soon enough, you will see more and more pollinators, and their presence will attract birds, both insect-eating and seed-eating species. Yes, some of them are eating the very pollinators that you have worked so hard to attract. But that's how nature works. You will have helped to improve the quality of life in large way, because a diversity and abundance of birds reflects a healthy ecosystem, and that's the goal.

APPENDIX A

Honey Bees

Honey bees (*Apis mellifera*) are probably the first insects that come to mind when you hear the word "pollinator." There is a good reason for this. Honey bees are the subject of many books, magazine articles, and television programs. And they are extremely important to modern agriculture. In the past few decades, agricultural enterprises have consolidated and grown enormously in scale, clearing away native bee habitat and increasing their dependence on honey bee pollination. Until recently honey bees were the only insect pollinator that could be trucked in by the millions to flowering fields, although this has changed for some crops with the success of mass rearings of the alfalfa leafcutter bee (*Megachile rotundata*) and certain bumble bees (*Bombus* spp.) that are now used to pollinate greenhouse tomatoes, peppers, and eggplants.

The honey bee is not, however, native to the Americas. It is a Eurasian and African species, originally brought to this continent by European settlers as a source of honey; in the last four centuries it has successfully spread throughout North America.

The *Pollinator Conservation Handbook* does not specifically address the conservation of the honey bee because it is an introduced species that did not evolve with the native flora and fauna. Honey bees, like native bees, are facing decline and require protection. However, they have the support of an active community of researchers, extension agents, inspectors, and beekeepers—both professional and amateur—and their representative organizations (the American Beekeeping Federation, for example). All of them are seeking solutions to the problems—primarily infectious disease, two introduced species of parasitic mites, and the volatile wholesale price of honey—that are responsible for honey bee declines. Although this support structure has been challenged in recent years by significant cuts in funding for both honey bee research and price supports for honey, the combined efforts and resources of these people and organizations amount to a considerable constituency for the honey bee. In contrast, there is very little support for research about the thousands of native bee species. The Xerces Society and The Bee Works are two of the few organizations that seek to understand and address their needs.

Honey bees have also been excluded from detailed discussion in the *Pollinators Conservation Handbook* because there are important questions about their role in the declining populations of native bee species. Over the past several years, studies have sought evidence to determine whether honey bees forage at the expense of native bees. This evidence has proved inconclusive. One reason is that there are few, if any, areas of North America to which the honey bee has not spread, so comparative studies with sites that are free of honey bees are nearly impossible to conduct. In addition, scientists studying insect ecology must contend with significant natural variations in climate, available pollen and nectar, and usable nest sites, as well as other constraints on populations of native bees, such as disease, predation, and parasitism. All of these factors may impact the number of native bees in an area, making it difficult to isolate the extent to which honey bees may be responsible for declines in native bee populations.

However, it is well known that the workers in just a single hive of honey bees may collect hundreds of pounds of nectar and tens of pounds of pollen in the course of a year. While we do not have a clear picture of whether the supply of nectar or pollen is limiting populations of bees, certainly it is hard to imagine that the presence of honey bees would not affect native bees living in the same area if there is limited forage available.

Finally, honey bees are less effective than native bees at pollinating some North American native plants, including various members of the heath and nightshade families. Thus, such plants may set fewer seeds when visited by honey bees than they would if visited by the wide diversity of native bees.

In light of the uncertainties about the impact of honey bees on native plant communities and native bees, we recommend a precautionary approach, in which managers of natural areas discourage the placement of honey bee hives, especially where there is unique or rare habitat. This restriction won't greatly impact the beekeeping community, and it may help conserve rare species of native bees, as well as the rare and endangered plants that depend upon native pollinators. In 2001 Region Three of the U.S. Fish and Wildlife Service, comprising eight upper-Midwest states, established a policy that would "err on the side of ecological caution" by excluding honey bee hives from National Wildlife Refuges throughout the region unless yields of a Refuge crop were dependent on them.

Furthermore, we believe that in agricultural settings, which for years have depended upon the timely placement of a dwindling number of honey bee hives in order to produce high yields, native bee habitat should be cultivated and protected. Researcher Claire Kremen of Princeton University has studied the important roles of native bees and their habitat in California agriculture, and concluded that their contribution could become "a valuable insurance policy if honey bees become more scarce or fail altogether."

Our decision to focus on the protection of native pollinator insects has been well considered. Our hope is that the information we provide on a wide variety of actions that you can take, together with resources for obtaining additional information, will enhance populations of native pollinators. In all likelihood, honey bees, not to mention the rest of the natural world, will fare better for your efforts.

Ideas for Educators and Parents

The creation of pollinator habitat is a wonderful project that can be used—in a school curriculum, with youth groups in local parks, or with your own children in your back yard—to develop skills in observation, techniques of scientific inquiry, mapping, graphing, problem solving, critical thinking, drawing, and a host of other subjects. Many activities can be done at minimal expense with little equipment; they require only time, patience, and a note pad.

Pollinators are easy to find and fun to observe in their daily lives: choosing flowers, collecting pollen and nectar, making nests, searching for mates. They are usually very focused creatures, not easily distracted from their attention to flowers, so you can watch them without disturbing them or affecting their behavior.

The lives of pollinators are also inextricably connected with those of flowering plants; these fascinating relationships open up many questions related to the evolution and adaptation of plants and animals.

Two good resources for suggestions and guidance are *Techniques for Pollination Biologists*, by Kearns and Inouye, and *The Natural History of Bumblebees: A Sourcebook for Investigations*, by Kearns and Thomson. Bibliographic information on both books is provided in Appendix C, which also suggests web sites that offer complete lesson plans and models for activities for children.

THE DATING GAME

Flowers that rely on insect pollinators need them to carry pollen from the anthers of one flower and move it to just the right place on the stigma of another.

- How is this achieved? Examine a flower with a magnifying glass or under a microscope. Where are the stamens and anthers? Can you find the greenish or orange marking that usually indicates the sugar-secreting nectary? Does the flower have a scent?

- Which insects visit which kinds of flowers? How long do they stay on each flower? What do they do on the flower? Do they collect pollen and nectar, sit around, fly around the plant? Are they always rewarded? Do they visit more than one bloom on each plant? Do they visit blooms on a single plant in a regular pattern?

- Do the insects have particular physical features (hairs, body shape, tongue length, etc.) to help them take nectar and pollen?

- Appendix C lists books and web sites that will help you to identify insects to species level, a task that can be challenging even for professional entomologists. Being able to identify an insect, if only to the level of family or genus, is valuable for pollinator studies.

FOOL A BEE

You can make artificial flowers that bees, flies, or butterflies will visit, and use them to isolate and test which factors—color, shape, or scent —attract different pollinators.

- Cut discs of different colors of paper or plastic and stick them onto a green background. Or cut out individual petals and arrange them to make flowers of different shapes or with varying numbers of petals, arranging them as complete flowers or as partial flowers with petals missing. What insects are attracted to the flowers? How long do they stay? What colors do they visit? Is there a pattern? Does one color attract more visitors in general, or only a single group of pollinators (for example, mostly bees or butterflies)?

- Stick the plastic discs or petals onto the underside of the cup of a golf tee and "plant" these in your grass or a tray of sand. Pour a little sugar water (one part sugar and two parts water, mixed together) into some of them. Do the bees visit those more regularly? Clean the flowers and put the sugar water in different flowers. Do the bees visit these now, or keep going to the flowers that used to have sugar water? What happens if you add artificial floral scents or perfumes to your artificial blossoms?

UNDERCOVER INVESTIGATION

What if there are no pollinators to pollinate the flowers? You can test this by preventing pollinators from reaching some flowers, and then comparing the fruit or seed that are set by the plants with flowers that were not visited by pollinators with those set by plants that were.

- Choose three or four similar plants and tie fine mesh bags over individual buds or entire plants. (See *Techniques for Pollination Biologists* for detailed instructions.) To record the development of individual flowers and fruit, you can mark individual buds with small paper tags (often sold as "jewelry tags").

- After the flowers have bloomed, collect the seed pods from the bagged and unbagged flowers or plants, and count the number of seeds inside each, or gather the fruit and examine its quality. Is there a significant difference between the number of seeds or the size and shape of the fruit produced by the bagged flowers and those produced by flowers that were not bagged? How else might flowers be pollinated?

INSIDE JOB

Everywhere you go you will find food that is the product of the work of a pollinator. Have you wondered how the flowers that produced these fruits look? Or what the inside of an apple looks like? What happens to fruit when the flower didn't get fully pollinated?

- Visit the grocery store, the library, or your own kitchen, and prepare a list of as many different fruits and vegetables as you can.

Which of these do you think needs to be pollinated? Find photographs of the flowers of these fruits and vegetables. What colors are the flowers? What structure do they have? Can you see the stamens and pistils? Which flowers depend upon insects for pollination and which depend upon the wind?

♦ Cut an apple or other fruit in half by slicing across it, halfway between the stem and the bottom. In the center of the apple there should be a star made up of five small compartments. These are the carpels, in which you will find seeds. There should be two seeds per carpel. How many seeds does your apple have? What shape is the fruit? How would you describe the inside of a peach? A raspberry? A strawberry? How does the number of seeds relate to the structure of the flower?

♦ Visit a berry farm or an apple or pear orchard. Are all the blueberries or pears the same size and color? Are some smaller or a different shape? Do you think enough pollinators visited the flowers? When you finish picking, eat some fruit. Do large, evenly shaped fruit taste any different from small, oddly shaped ones?

Congratulations, It's a . . . Caterpillar!

Caterpillars are easy to raise in a cage in your classroom, home, or yard, and fun to watch as they grow, molt several times, and then finally pupate.

♦ A rearing cage can be made easily with two quilting rings (14 inches in diameter is a good size) and two yards of tulle fabric. Wrap the fabric around the quilting rings to form a cylinder and close it with knots at the top and bottom. Overlap the fabric by at least six inches at the back; you will be able to reach into the cage via this overlapping area, but butterflies should not be able to get out. (For added security, fasten the fabric with a binder clip or two.) This cage can be hung from the ceiling, in a garden gazebo, or on a tree, where you can easily watch it.

- Search the plants in your garden or school grounds for caterpillars to bring inside. (Although you can buy kits with caterpillars in them, this is not recommended; those caterpillars are probably bred from butterflies native to a region of the country other than your own, and when the adults are released they may cause problems for the local, native populations, even if they are the same species. It is much better to find local caterpillars.) The species of plant on which you find the caterpillars will likely be the host plant that you should put in the cage. How fast do the caterpillars grow? How many times do they molt their skin, and what happens to the old one? Is each instar the same shape and color? What do you notice about their behaviors? What happens when they pupate? How does the butterfly emerge from the chrysalis?

DOMESTIC STUDIES

Nesting sites for wood-nesting bees will provide hours of fascinating viewing and offer many teaching opportunities.

- Which holes are being used? How long are the bees away from the nest, foraging? What do they carry back to the nest: leaf pieces, mud, resin, pollen? Does their behavior vary depending on what they are carrying? How long do they spend inside the holes?

- Note when the nesting site was first used. When was the most recent activity? Were there periods when nothing was happening?

- Are all the occupants the same? Did you notice any parasitic wasps, flies, or bees around the nest entrances?

- Similar observations can be made for ground-nesting sites, although sometimes it is harder to watch individual nest entrances. A clear plastic cup placed over a hole will temporarily stop bees from leaving or entering, so that you can better see and time their movements. With a cup in place you can also count how many bees exit a hole. Are they solitary or social bees?

APPENDIX C

Resources

The *Pollinator Conservation Handbook* is intended to be a starting point for your pollinator discoveries. In this appendix you will find listed some of our favorite books, web sites, and other resources to help you explore in more detail and depth the valuable, amazing, and entertaining world of pollinators.

The first two sections, listing books and web sites, are each divided into three categories: "Biology and Conservation," "Plant-Pollinator Relationships," and "Educational Ideas and Pollinator Identification." The third section lists nonprofit organizations and companies involved with pollinator insect conservation. In selecting web sites to list, we have focused on ones that are well established as of the summer of 2003, and that we therefore believe are likely to be useful and accessible for some time.

Four of the books listed may be considered our essential book list for anyone wanting to better understand pollinators and their biology. *The Forgotten Pollinators*, by Buchmann and Nabhan, and *The Natural History of Pollination*, by Procter, Yeo, and Lack, provide detailed overviews of pollination; and *The Natural History of Bumblebees*, by Kearns and Thomson, and *Bees of the World*, by O'Toole and Raw, cover the biology of bees. Other books we strongly recommend are Michener's magnificent *The Bees of the World* and Scott's *The Butterflies of North America*, which give great detail of their subjects but are expensive; and *Techniques for Pollination Biologists*, by Kearns and Inouye, which due to its specialized subject will not be relevant for everybody.

Regional field guides for insects and plants are not listed. They are an essential resource, but it is not possible to adequately list all the publications covering all regions within the United States. For field guides and other information appropriate to your area, we suggest that you contact your local library, book store, garden store, or native plant society.

BOOKS

Biology and Conservation

Boring, J. K., E. Glasener, G. Keator, J. Knopf, J. Scott, and S. Wasowski. 1995. *Natural Gardening*. Time Life Books, New York, NY. This book provides advice on choosing plants for natural gardens in a format that makes it easy to find information for your region.

Buchmann, S. L., and G. P. Nabhan. 1997. *The Forgotten Pollinators*. Island Press, Washington, D.C. An excellent introduction to all aspects of pollinators and pollination. A highly recommended book and a call to arms for pollinator conservation and habitat restoration.

Cranshaw, W. 1998. *Pests of the West*. Second edition. Fulcrum Publishing, Golden, CO. Contains information on prevention and control measures for insect pests for gardens and small farms, including a chapter on the importance of soil to a healthy garden.

Ellis, B. W., F. M. Bradley, H. Atthowe, and R. Yepsen. 1996. *The Organic Gardeners Handbook of Natural Insect and Disease Control*. Rodale Press, Inc., Emmaus, PA. Provides basic information, with entries on more than two hundred plants and their cultivation, soil preparation methods, pests, garden plans, etc.

Emmel, T. C. 1997. *Butterfly Gardening: Creating a Butterfly Haven in Your Garden*. Friedman / Fairfax Publishers, New York, NY. A great introduction to butterfly gardening that is full of practical advice.

Griffin, B. L. 1999. *The Orchard Mason Bee*. Second edition. Knox Cellars Publishing, Bellingham, WA. A jargon-free book about the blue orchard bee.

Jackson, B., and V. Baines. 1999. *Mindful of Butterflies*. The Book Guild, Lewes, U.K. A beautifully illustrated book with comprehensive information on all aspects of gardening for and rearing butterflies.

Johansen, C. A., and D. F. Meyer. 1990. *Pollinator Protection: A Bee & Pesticide Handbook*. Wicwas Press, Cheshire, U.K. Information on a highly technical subject presented in a very readable way.

Jones, R., and P. Munn, eds. 1998. *Habitat Management For Wild Bees and Wasps*. International Bee Research Association, Cardiff, U.K. A good introduction to various aspects of bee conservation, including a chapter on bee surveys.

Kearns, C., and J. Thomson. 2001. *The Natural History of Bumblebees: A Sourcebook for Investigations*. University Press of Colorado, Boulder, CO. This slim, highly readable, and highly recommended book offers an excellent introduction to bumble bees, covering their biology and conservation, and some research activities.

Matheson, A., ed. 1994. *Forage For Bees In An Agricultural Landscape*. International Bee Research Association, Cardiff, U.K. Advice on how to provide sources of nectar and pollen for bees.

Matheson, A., S. L. Buchmann, C. O'Toole, P. Westrich, and I. H. Williams, eds. 1996. *The Conservation of Bees*. Linnean Society Symposium Series, Number 18. Academic Press, Harcourt Brace & Company, London and New York, NY. An excellent compilation of several papers discussing different components of bee conservation, including the ecological basis for conservation, habitat management, and honey bee competition.

Mayer, D. F., C. A. Johansen, and C. R. Baird. 1999. *How to Reduce Bee Poisoning from Pesticides*. Pacific Northwest Extension Publication 518. Washington State University, Prosser, WA. A booklet with extensive tables listing pesticides and their toxicity to bees. It is available as a PDF file from cru.cahe.wsu.edu/CEPublications/pnw0518/pnw0518.pdf.

O'Neill, K. 2001. *Solitary Wasps: Behavior and Natural History*. Cornell University Press, Ithaca, NY. An excellent book on solitary wasps, who share many habitat and behavioral traits with bees.

O'Toole, C., and A. Raw. 1999. *Bees of the World*. Blandford, London, U.K. A comprehensive introduction to bee biology, behaviors, and life cycles. If you are going to buy one book on bees, this is it.

Pesticide Action Network. 2000. *Hooked on Poison: Pesticide Use in California, 1991–1998*. Pesticide Action Network North America, San Francisco, CA. This analysis of pesticide use in Californian homes, gardens, and farmland is also available online at www.panna.org/resources/documents/hookedAvail.dv.html.

Xerces Society and Smithsonian Institution. 1998. *Butterfly Gardening: Creating Summer Magic in Your Garden*. Sierra Club Books, San Francisco, CA. This book contains detailed advice on all aspects of creating and managing gardens for butterflies, moths, and other beneficial insects; each chapter is written by an acknowledged expert.

Plant-Pollinator Relationships

Barth, F. G. 1985. *Insects and Flowers: The Biology of a Partnership*. Princeton University Press, Princeton, NJ. A good discussion of how insects—mostly honey bees—and flowers are adapted to each other.

Bosch, J., and W. Kemp. 2001. *How to Manage the Blue Orchard Bee As an Orchard Pollinator*. The National Outreach Arm of USDA-SARE, Handbook Series, Book 5., Sustainable Agriculture Network, National Agricultural Library, Beltsville, MD. A good guide to managing the blue orchard bee—also called the orchard mason bee—as a reliable pollinator.

Delaplane, K. S., and D. F. Mayer. 2000. *Crop Pollination by Bees*. CAB International, Wallingford, U.K. Separate chapters cover the biology of different commercially used pollinators, how to achieve effective pollination of crops, and the conservation of bees.

Free, J. 1992. *Insect Pollination of Cultivated Crops*. Academic Press, London, U.K. Detailed information on the pollination requirements of different crops.

McGregor, S. E. 1976. *Insect Pollination Of Cultivated Crop Plants*. USDA Carl Hayden Bee Research Center, Tucson, AZ. A detailed guide to the pollination requirements of a wide range of crops, but a bit out of date. It can be read only on the Carl Hayden Bee Research Center's web site, at gears.tucson.ars.ag.gov/book/index.html.

Procter, M., P. Yeo, and A. Lack. 1996. *The Natural History of Pollination*. Timber Press, Portland, OR. Probably the best single volume on pollination and plant-pollinator relationships.

Educational Ideas and Pollinator Identification

Bland, R. G., and H. E. Jaques. 1978. *How To Know The Insects*. McGraw-Hill, New York, NY. Originally published over half a century ago, this is in its most recent edition still a good introduction to insect identification.

Borror, D. J., and R. E. White. 1998. *A Field Guide to Insects: America North of Mexico*. Houghton Mifflin, Boston, MA. A comprehensive, easy-to-follow guide for identifying commonly seen insects.

Glassberg, J. 1999 and 2001, respectively. *Butterflies Through Binoculars: East* and *Butterflies Through Binoculars: West*. Oxford University Press, New York, NY. Easy-to-follow photographic guides to butterflies of the eastern and western United States.

Imes, R. 1992. *The Practical Entomologist*. Fireside Books, New York, NY. An introductory book full of practical information, including on how to collect and rear insects.

Kearns, C. A., and D. Inouye. 1993. *Techniques for Pollination Biologists*. University Press of Colorado, Niwot, CO. Comprehensive guidance on how to plan and implement pollination studies, from simple monitoring of flower visits to lab techniques for pollen analysis. Covers methods—from basic to advanced—for capturing insects, removing pollen, covering plants or flowers, cross-pollinating flowers, and making artificial flowers. Also covers more advanced skills like pollen analysis and other lab-based studies that may be more appropriate for high school or college students.

Michener, C. D. 2000. *The Bees of the World.* Johns Hopkins University Press, Baltimore, MD. If you are serious about bees, this is a book you will want to read. Written by the world's pre-eminent bee researcher, it includes excellent essays on bee biology and keys that—with practice and a microscope—will enable you to identify any bee to subgenus level.

Michener, C. D., R. J. McGinley, and B. N. Danforth. 1994. *The Bee Genera of North and Central America (Hymenoptera:Apoidea).* Smithsonian Institution Press, Washington, D.C. Written in both English and Spanish, the key will enable you to identify North American bees to the genus level. It includes a brief note on each genera. A fantastic resource that takes practice to use effectively.

Milne, L. J. 1980. *National Audubon Society Field Guide to Insects and Spiders of North America.* Alfred A. Knopf, New York, NY. A photographic guide to a wide range of insects.

Pyle, R. M. 1992. *Handbook for Butterfly Watchers.* Houghton Mifflin, New York. An introduction to observing and understanding butterflies, with chapters rearing them and on gardening.

Schauff, M. E., ed. Undated. *Collecting and Preserving Insects and Mites: Techniques and Tools.* USDA Systematic Entomology Laboratory, Washington, D.C. Offering detailed guidance on field and laboratory techniques, this is available online only as a PDF file, at www.sel.barc.usda.gov/selhome/collpres/collpres.htm.

Scott, J. A. 1986. *The Butterflies of North America: A Natural History and Field Guide.* Stanford University Press, Stanford, CA. This book is a valuable source of information on the continent's butterflies.

INTERNET SITES

Biology and Conservation

The Bee Works. Conservation advice, plus education ideas; www.the beeworks.com.

The Bumblebee Pages. www.mearns.org.uk/mrssmith/bees/index.htm

The Children's Butterfly Site. www.mesc.nbs.gov/resources/education/ butterfly/bfly_start.asp.

Conservation Ecology, an online journal. Special issue on pollinator conservation; www.consecol.org/vol5/iss1/index.html.

Ecological Society of America's "Pollination Tool Kit." Information on the science behind pollinator conservation and United States legislation; www.esa.org/ecoservices/.

National Wildlife Federation. Backyard wildlife habitat; www.nwf.org/ backyardwildlifehabitat/.

Native Plants Network. Information on growing plants from seed; nativeplants.for.uidaho.edu/.

University of Wisconsin, Madison. A list of bumble bee plants; www. cae.wisc.edu/~oliphant/bees/bombus/pollination.shtml.

USDA Bee Biology and Systematics Laboratory, Logan Utah. Information on bee plants (both native and garden) and making nests, and an extensive list of suppliers of bees, tubes, and nests; www. loganbeelab.usu.edu/default.htm.

The Xerces Society. Bee biology, conservation advice, butterfly gardening, and links; www.xerces.org/poll/index.htm.

Plant-Pollinator Relationships

Insect Visitors of Prairie Wildflowers in Illinois. www.shout.net/~ jhilty/.

Pollination Home Page. A web site with plenty of information on bees, bee keeping, and crop pollination; www.pollinator.com.

USDA Agricultural Research Service. An article on alternative pollinators; www.ars.usda.gov/is/AR/archive/may00/buzz0500.htm.

Educational Ideas and Pollinator Identification

Bumble Boosters, a project of the University of Nebraska, Lincoln. Bumble bee biology, an interactive identification key, and education activities for high school students; bumbleboosters.unl.edu/.

Bee Eye. A simulation of how a bee sees; cvs.anu.edu.au/andy/beye/beyehome.html.

Canadian Biodiversity Institute. Ways to create habitat in school grounds; www.schoolgrounds.ca/schoolgrounds/home.html.

Discover Life. Resources to help study wildlife, including keys to identify bumble bees and some butterflies; www.discoverlife.org.

Green Teacher / Green Brick Road. Environmental education resources on line; weblinks.schoolsgogreen.org/links/weblinks_schlgrnd/.

Insect Safari. Activities and lesson plans for students from kindergarten to grade five; www.insectsafari.com/home.asp.

Insect World. Information on all sorts of pollinators; www.earthlife. net/insects/six.html.

Journey North. Information on migrating wildlife, including monarch butterflies, and ways to participate in the seasonal tracking program; www.learner.org/jnorth/.

Northern Prairies Wildlife Resource Center. Photographic guides to butterfly and moth identification, listed state by state, plus biology notes on each species; www.npwrc.usgs.gov/resource/distr/lepid/bflyusa/bflyusa.htm and www.npwrc.usgs.gov/resource/distr/lepid/moths/mothsusa.htm.

Smithsonian Institution. Pollination lesson plans for grades four to nine; www.smithsonianeducation.org/educators/lesson_plans/partners_in_pollination/index.html.

Nonprofit Organizations and Companies

The Bee Works. Environmental consultancy engaged in native bee research and conservation efforts, pollinator surveys, GIS planning, mapping, and DAISY automated insect identification.
>1870 W Prince Road, Suite 16, Tucson, AZ 85705
>Telephone: 520-888-7422; Fax: 520-888-7332
>Web site: www.thebeeworks.com
>E-mail: info@thebeeworks.com

BioQuip. Supplier of entomological equipment, books, and materials.
>2321 Gladwick Street, Rancho Dominguez, CA 90220
>Telephone: 310-667-8800; Fax: 310-667-8808
>Web site: www.bioquip.com

Carolina Biological Supply Company. Supplier of science and educational equipment.
>2700 York Road, Burlington, NC 27215
>Telephone: 800-334-5551; Fax: 800-222-7112
>Web site: www.carolina.com

Entomo-Logic. Company that offers technical advice on commercial pollination and supplies blue orchard bees.
>21323 232nd Street SE, Monroe, WA 98272
>Telephone: 360-863-8547
>E-mail: entomologic@seanet.com

Knox Cellars. Company that sells blue orchard bees and nesting supplies for these and bumble bees.
>1607 Knox Avenue, Bellingham, WA 98225
>Telephone: 425-898-8802; Fax: 425-898-8070
>Web site: www.knoxcellars.com

Lady Bird Johnson Wildflower Center. Nonprofit center that is a great resource for native plant information. Can supply lists of suitable plant species for many areas.

> 4801 La Crosse Avenue, Austin, TX 78739
> Telephone: 512-292-4200; Fax: 512-292-4627
> Web site: www.wildflower.org

Monarch Watch. An educational outreach program of the University of Kansas that promotes the conservation of monarch butterflies and education activities about the fall migration.

> University of Kansas
> 1200 Sunnyside Avenue, Lawrence, KS 66045
> Telephone: 888-TAGGING or 785-864-4441
> Fax: 785-864-5321
> Web site: www.monarchwatch.org

National Gardening Association. Nonprofit that helps gardeners and helps people through gardening.

> 1100 Dorset Street, South Burlington, VT 05403
> Telephone: 802-863-5251; Fax: 802-864-6889
> Web site: www.garden.org

Native Plant Society. Nonprofit that encourages conservation of native plants. The web site of the Lady Bird Johnston Wildflower Center (www.wildflower.org) lists all the state societies.

North American Pollinator Protection Campaign. Consortium of conservation groups, government agencies, universities, and private industries from the United States, Mexico, and Canada, who share information and work together for the good of pollinators.

> 423 Washington Street, 4th Floor
> San Francisco, CA 94111
> Telephone: 415-362-1137; Fax: 415-362-3070
> Web site: www.nappc.org

Northwest Coalition for Alternatives to Pesticides. Nonprofit that works to protect people and the environment by advancing healthy solutions to pest problems.

> P.O. Box 1393, Eugene, OR 97440
> Telephone: 541-344-5044; Fax: 541-344-6923
> Web site: www.pesticide.org

Pesticide Action Network North America. Nonprofit that works to replace pesticide use with ecologically sound and socially just alternatives.

> 49 Powell St., Suite 500, San Francisco, CA 94102
> Telephone: 415-981-1771; Fax: 415-981-1991
> Web site: www.panna.org

Pollinator Paradise. Company that sells nesting blocks, provides consultancy services, and undertakes research on bee conservation and management for agriculture.

> 31140 Circle Drive, Parma, ID 83660
> Telephone: 208-722-7808
> Web site: www.pollinatorparadise.com

Wildlife Habitat Council. Nonprofit that helps large landowners, particularly corporations, manage their unused lands in an ecologically sensitive manner for the benefit of wildlife.

> 8737 Colesville Road, Suite 800, Silver Spring, MD 20910
> Telephone: 301-588-8994; Fax: 301-588-4629
> Web site: www.wildlifehc.org

The Xerces Society. Nonprofit dedicated to preserving the diversity of life through the conservation of invertebrates. Its Pollinator Conservation Program offers practical advice on the conservation of pollinator insects.

> 4828 SE Hawthorne Boulevard, Portland, OR 97215
> Telephone: 503-232-6639; Fax: 503-233-6794
> Web site: www.xerces.org

APPENDIX D
Plant Lists

In this appendix we provide three plant lists to help you select appropriate plants to satisfy the foraging needs of some pollinators. Because you will want to use the species of plant that is native to your locale, we list plants by genus; a regional wildflower guide or your local nursery can help you select the plants suitable for your particular area.

List 1 includes genera of native plants that contain "bee-friendly" species and would be appropriate in any planting situation from a back yard garden to a wild area. It is by no means exhaustive; in deciding which genera to list, we have struck a balance between including those that offer food to a wide range of pollinator insects and avoiding those whose distributions are limited to small regions. Use this list as a starting point.

List 2 includes genera of non-native plants that also contain "bee-friendly" species but would be appropriate only in yard or garden settings. These plants should not be planted in "natural" or wild areas. The older—or heirloom—varieties of the plants are preferred; for more information, it is again best to consult a local nursery.

Butterfly host plants—plants that provide the food source for caterpillars and on which the females lay their eggs—are a vital component of pollinator habitat. List 3 includes genera of host plants for some common butterflies. Again, this list is not exhaustive. Other sources of host-plant information include butterfly gardening books and field guides; some titles are included in Appendix C.

1: NATIVE PLANTS PROVIDING NECTAR AND POLLEN

Perennial Herbaceous Plants

Genus	Common Name
Abutilon	Indian mallow
Achillea	yarrow
Agastache	giant hyssop
Agave	agave century plant
Allium	wild onion wild leek wild garlic
Anaphalis	pearly everlasting
Argemone	prickly poppy
Artemisia	sagebrush wormwood
Aster	aster
Brodiaea	brodiaea
Castilleja	paint brush
Chamerion	fireweed
Cirsium	thistle
Coreopsis	tickseed coreopsis
Daucus	wild carrot rattlesnake weed
Delphinium	larkspur
Dodecatheon	shooting star mosquito bills
Echinacea	coneflower
Erigeron	fleabane daisy
Eriogonum	buckwheat

Genus	Common Name
Erysimum	wallflower
	prairie rocket
Eschscholzia	California poppy
	golden poppy
Eupatorium	Joe-pye weed
	thoroughwort
Gaillardia	blanket flower
	firewheel
Geranium	geranium
	cranesbill
Geum	avens
	prairie smoke
Helianthus	sunflower
	blueweed
Heracleum	cow parsnip
Hieracium	hawkweed
Ipomoea	morning glory
	scarlet creeper
	railway vine
Kallstroemia	caltrop
	Arizona poppy
Liatris	blazing star
	gayfeather
Linum	flax
Lomatium	desert parsley
	lomatium
	biscuitroot
Lupinus	lupine
Oenothera	evening primrose
Papaver	poppy
Penstemon	penstemon
	beardtongue

Genus	Common Name
Phacelia	phacelia scorpion weed
Rudbeckia	coneflower black-eyed Susan
Salvia	sage
Scutellaria	skullcap
Sedum	stonecrop
Senecio	butterweed groundsel ragwort
Solanum	nightshade horsenettle
Solidago	goldenrod
Sphaeralcea	globe mallow
Verbena	verbena
Zinnia	zinnia

Annual and Biennial Herbaceous Plants

Genus	Common Name
Argemone	prickly poppy
Asclepias	milkweed
Bidens	beggar ticks
Cirsium	thistle
Clarkia	clarkia fairyfan farewell to spring
Cleome	bee plant spider flower
Cosmos	cosmos
Erigeron	fleabane daisy

Genus	Common Name
Eriogonum	buckwheat
Gilia	gilia
	gily flower
Ipomoea	morning glory
Linum	flax
Lupinus	lupine
Nemophila	baby blue eyes
	blue eyes
Oenothera	evening primrose
Papaver	poppy
Phacelia	phacelia
	scorpion weed
Salvia	sage
Verbascum	mullein
Verbena	verbena
Zinnia	zinnia

Trees and Shrubs

Genus	Common Name
Amelanchier	serviceberry
	sugarplum
Arbutus	madrone
Artemisia	sagebrush
	wormwood
Berberis	barberry
Ceanothus	ceanothus
	California lilac
	New Jersey tea
	buckbrush
Chilopsis	desert willow
Chrysothamnus	rabbitbrush

Genus	Common Name
Crataegus	hawthorn
Larrea	creosote bush
Mahonia	Oregon grape barberry mahonia
Monarda	bee balm horsemint oswego tea
Opuntia	cholla prickly pear
Prunus	chokecherry plum cherry desert almond
Rhododendron	rhododendron azalea
Rhus	sumac
Ribes	currant gooseberry
Rosa	wild rose
Rubus	blackberry salmonberry raspberry dewberry
Salix	willow
Sambucus	elder elderberry
Symphoricarpos	snowberry coralberry
Vaccinium	huckleberry blueberry bilberry

2: Non-Native Plants Providing Nectar and Pollen

Perennial Herbaceous Plants

Genus	Common Name
Chrysanthemum	daisy
Echinops	globe thistle
Lavandula	English lavender
Lotus	bird's-foot trefoil
Mentha	mint
Ocimum	basil
Origanum	marjoram
Papaver	poppy
Rosmarinus	rosemary
Thymus	thyme
Trifolium	clover

Annual and Biennial Herbaceous Plants

Genus	Common Name
Borago	borage
Hyssopus	hyssop
Melilotus	sweet clover
Malva	mallow
Papaver	poppy
Verbascum	mullein

Trees and Shrubs

Genus	Common Name
Cotoneaster	cotoneaster
Lantana	lantana yellow sage
Malus	apple
Pyrus	pear

3: Larval Host Plants for Some Common Butterflies

In addition to plants in the genera listed below, grasses and sedges of various genera serve as host plants for many species of butterfly, including skippers.

Larval Host Plants

Genus	Common Name	Butterflies
Asclepias	milkweed	monarch, queen
Astragalus	milk vetch	blues
Barbarea	winter cress	whites and blues
Castilleja	paint brush	checkerspots
Cirsium	thistle	painted lady
Daucus	wild carrot	swallowtails
Foeniculum	fennel	swallowtails
Lupinus	lupines	blues
Passiflora	passion flower	gulf fritillary, heliconian
Petroselinum	parsley	swallowtails
Plantago	plantain	buckeye, checkerspots
Populus	aspen	many species
Prunus	cherry, plum	swallowtails, hairstreaks
Rosa	rose	mourning cloak
Salix	willow	many species
Spiraea	spirea	many species
Trifolium	clover	sulfurs and blues
Urtica	nettle	anglewings, red admiral
Viola	violets	fritillaries
Vicia	vetch	sulphurs and blues

Glossary

Abdomen. The hindmost of an insect's three body segments, in which most vital organs are located.

Anther. The part of a flower's stamen that bears the pollen.

Aposematic coloration. Bright, conspicuous markings on stinging, poisonous, or distasteful animals, which predators learn to avoid.

Bee bread. A mixture of nectar and pollen left in the brood cell by the female bees to be consumed by her offspring.

Brood cell. A chamber in a bee nest in which a larva develops. For most bees, the brood cell contains a single egg and is sealed by the female bee after provisioning. Bumble bees lay several eggs in one cell and may provision it gradually as the larvae grow.

Carpel. The part of a flower that contains the ovary, within which the seeds will develop after pollination.

Caterpillar. The larval stage of butterflies and moths.

Chrysalis. The pupal stage of butterflies and moths.

Cleptoparasite. A bee species that does not make its own nest, but instead lays its eggs in the nests of another species so that its offspring can eat the food provisions intended for the host larvae.

Cocoon. A silk case, made by a caterpillar before it pupates, in which most moths and some butterflies spend their time as a chrysalis.

Co-evolution. The process of evolution in which two or more species contribute reciprocally to the forces of natural selection.

Coleoptera. The insect order that includes beetles and weevils. The adults are characterized by having forewings hardened to form elytra, which can be closed to make a protective layer over their backs. Translated from its Greek origins, it means "sheath wings."

Corbicula (plural *corbiculae*); also known as a *pollen basket*. The structure formed by long, stiff, inward curved hairs surrounding a smooth area on the hind leg of some bees (primarily bumble bees and honey bees), and used to carry pollen moistened with nectar.

Cuckoo bee. A cleptoparasite that lays its eggs in the nests of solitary bees.

Diapause. A delay in insect development that is not directly caused by environmental conditions.

Diptera. The insect order that contains flies. The adults are characterized by having one pair of wings; translated from its Greek origins, Diptera means "two wings."

Elytra (singular *elytron*). The hardened forewings of a beetle, which form a protective shell when closed across its back. In some flightless beetles, the elytra are fused and cannot be opened.

Eruption. A seasonal expansion in the range of some butterflies caused by heavy population pressure in their core breeding areas.

Family. A group of organisms that share recognizable features of common descent. The family name is always printed in regular type and capitalized, and often ends in –idae; for example, Megachilidae is the family that includes leafcutter bees and mason bees.

Foraging. The action by an adult insect of gathering food or nesting materials for itself or its offspring.

Fruit. The fleshy part of the carpel that develops with the seed.

Gamete. The mature, functional reproductive cells of a plant. A plant has both male and female gametes, which must join to effect fertilization and thus seed development.

Genus (plural *genera*). A group of closely related species. The genus is printed in italics and capitalized; for example, *Osmia* is the genus that includes the orchard mason bee.

Glossa (plural *glossae*). The final segment of a bee's tongue. In most long-tongued bees this is elongate and curled to form a tube.

Ground-nesting. Bees that make nests in the ground, usually by excavating a tunnel and a series of brood cells.

Head. The foremost of the three major body segments of insects.

Hemolymph. The watery fluid that carries nutrients through an insect's body. Hemolymph is, in effect, insect blood, but circulates in open tissue spaces and is not restricted to veins and arteries.

Hibernation. A dormant stage that many adult insects pass through to survive winter. The summer equivalent is "aestivation."

Host plant. A species of plant that a butterfly caterpillar will eat. The female must lay her eggs on or close to it.

Hymenoptera. The insect order that contains bees, wasps, sawflies, and ants, with adults characterized by biting and chewing mouthparts, two pairs of wings, and prominent antennae. Translated from its Greek origins, it means "membrane wings."

Imago (plural *imagines* or *imagos*). A fully developed adult insect.

Indicator species. A species (or group of species) whose presence or absence in an ecosystem can be used as a measure of its health.

Insect. An invertebrate animal that, as an adult, has three body parts (head, thorax, and abdomen), three pairs of jointed legs attached to the thorax, and usually two pairs of wings.

Instar. A stage in an insect's life history between molts.

Invasive species. A species that can out-compete, displace, or otherwise harm local species of plants and animals.

Keystone species. A species that is needed for the survival of other species in an ecosystem, and the loss of which would thus lead to the decline or disappearance of other species.

Larva (plural *larvae*). The young insect hatched from the egg. It differs completely from the adult in form and often in dietary needs.

Lepidoptera. The insect order that includes moths and butterflies. Translated from its Greek origins, it means "scale wings."

Metamorphosis. The process by which an insect changes in body form as it develops.

Mimic. A species that has evolved to resemble another. This may offer protection from predators for the mimic, as the model may sting.

Molt. The process by which a larva sheds its outer skin. Because the outer skin is inflexible and does not expand, a larva must molt in order to grow.

Monolectic. Bees that collect pollen from only one species of plant to provision their brood cells. The bee will usually collect nectar from a wider range of plants.

Native. A species of animal or plant that naturally occurs in a region.

Nectar. A sugar-rich fluid produced by flowers, which attracts pollinating animals.

Nectar corridor. Habitat along the migration route of a pollinator, either a continuous strip or "stepping stones," which provides foraging and refueling resources across an otherwise inhospitable landscape.

Nectar guides. Patterns of color markings on petals that direct flower visitors to nectar.

Non-native. A species of animal or plant that does not naturally occur in a region.

Oligolectic. Bees that collect pollen from a limited range of plants (often those in a single genus or family) to provision their brood cells. These bees will usually collect nectar from a wider range of plants.

Order. A group of families that have evolved from a common source. Orders are printed in regular type and capitalized. The four orders discussed in this handbook are Coleoptera, Diptera, Hymenoptera, and Lepidoptera.

Pistil. The female part of a flower, comprising the stigma, style, and carpel.

Pollen; also called ***pollen grains***. Microscopic, hard capsules containing the male gametes of a plant.

Pollination. The transfer of pollen grains from an anther to a receptive stigma. Self-pollination is movement within a flower or between flowers on the same plant; cross-pollination is between flowers on separate plants. Pollen may be carried by wind, water, or animals.

Pollinator. An animal that moves pollen and can effect pollination.

Polylectic. Bees that collect both pollen and nectar from a wide range of plants.

Prepupa (plural ***prepupae***). The final stage of the last larval instar. In bees, this is the stage after the larva has defecated; during unfavorable conditions a prepupa can remain dormant for extended periods.

Pupa (plural ***pupae***). A life stage of those insects that undergo complete metamorphosis. During this stage, as its body form changes from larva to adult, the insect is inactive.

Pupation. The act of becoming a pupa.

Queen. The egg-laying female in a social bee colony.

Scopa (plural *scopae*); also know as a ***pollen brush***. A patch of special hairs on a bee's body that are used to carry dry pollen back to the nest. Usually, the scopa is on the back legs, although in some families it is on the sides of the thorax or the underside of the abdomen

Seed. The part of a plant that contains the embryo, a protective coating, and stored food, and which can develop into a new plant.

Social. Insects that live in colonies and work together to build nests and to provide food for and raise their offspring. Only a few native bee species, including bumble bees and sweat bees, are social.

Social parasite. A parasitic bee that lives in—and lays its egg inside—the nests of social bees.

Solitary. Bees that, after mating, prepare and provision their own nests without cooperation with other bees. The great majority of bee species are solitary.

Species. Individuals that form a group, look more or less alike, and can breed freely among themselves to produce another generation of similar creatures. Abbreviated to sp. for one species and spp. for two or more species. The species name is always printed in italics and is not capitalized; for example, *lignaria*, the orchard mason bee species in the genus *Osmia*.

Stamen. The male part of a flower, comprising an anther on a filament. Often, many stamens form a ring around the center of a flower.

Stigma. The part of the carpel that is receptive to pollen and on which the pollen germinates.

Sub-lethal. The impact of pesticide poisoning that does not kill an insect but affects its ability to forage or nest. Sub-lethal effects may include agitated behavior, wobbly movements, or paralysis.

Subspecies. A geographically defined group that looks different from other groups of the same species, but can freely interbreed with them. Abbreviated to ssp. The subspecies name is always printed in italics and is not capitalized; for example, *propinqua*, the western subspecies of the orchard mason bee, *Osmia lignaria*).

Thorax. The central of an insect's three major body segments, and the one to which wings and legs are attached.

Ultraviolet. A color that has wavelengths too short to be seen by humans, but can be seen by bees.

Weed. Any undesirable plant, often one that grows in abundance to the detriment of plants you want.

Wood-nesting. Bees that construct nests in or on woody stems, twigs, and snags. Approximately 30 percent of bees are wood-nesting species, the majority occupying pre-existing holes.

Worker. A female bee in a social colony that does the foraging, nest construction, and tends the larvae. A worker does not lay eggs.

About the Authors

Matthew Shepherd heads the Xerces Society's pollinator conservation program. British by birth, he established a successful community-based conservation program and helped create an award-winning nature park in England. Matthew spent two years as a volunteer in Kenya, working with communities and government agencies to improve the management of the Arabuko-Sokoke Forest. He serves on the steering committee of the North American Pollinator Protection Campaign.

Stephen Buchmann directs The Bee Works, an environmental consulting company in Tucson specializing in pollinator surveys and GIS mapping. He is also CEO of Morpho, Inc., a software company whose product, DAISY, uses pattern recognition to identify, among other organisms, bees, butterflies, and moths. A graduate of the University of California at Davis, he has published over 150 articles and several books, including *The Forgotten Pollinators*, and serves on the steering committee of the North American Pollinator Protection Campaign.

Mace Vaughan, staff entomologist for the Xerces Society, earned his masters degrees in entomology and education from Cornell University. He has studied ground beetles in riparian forests of Utah and the behavior of honey bees in upstate New York, has wrangled insects for two PBS nature documentaries, and has taught a wide range of audiences across the United States about bees, spiders, and butterflies.

Scott Hoffman Black, the Xerces Society's executive director, has degrees in ecology, plant science, and entomology from Colorado State University. As a researcher, conservationist, and teacher, he has worked with small issues groups and large coalitions advocating science-based conservation. Scott has authored many scientific and popular publications and his work has been featured in newspaper articles, on radio and television, and in two books by the National Geographic Society.